A TRAVELER'S GUIDE TO RUBBER STAMP STORES

David Ward

Cornucopia Press
Seattle, Washington

A TRAVELER'S GUIDE TO RUBBER STAMP STORES

David Ward

Published by:

Cornucopia Press
4739 University Way NE
Suite 1610-B
Seattle, WA 98105
U.S.A.

Copyright © 1998 by David Ward

Second edition, completely revised

Printed in the United States

Publisher's Cataloging in Publication
(Prepared by Quality Books Inc.)

Ward, David.
   A traveler's guide to rubber stamp stores / David Ward.
   p. cm.
   Includes index.
   LCCN: 98-092761
   ISBN: 0-9641445-3-0

1. Rubber stamps—North America—Directories. 2. Rubber stamps—Europe—Directories. 3. Rubber stamp printing.   I. Title.

TT867.W365 1998   761
                                                        QBI98-1027

TABLE OF CONTENTS

ACKNOWLEDGMENTS

A variety of people doing many different jobs helped to make this book a reality.

David Scherzer and Moreah Vestan both did a wonderful job with the thankless task of entering large amounts of detailed information from the stores and kept the office running smoothly.

Paola Rubbo should be crowned "Queen of Graphic Arts" for her work on all the little nuances of type, layout, and design that made this book look good.

Putting this book together also required an immense amount of computer programming, not only for the production of the book but also for all the background systems needed for the business. Seth Ritemer performed miracles by combining over 100 fields of information from the listing, contacts, billing, and five other sources into one user-friendly computer screen, saving us hours of work. Bill Aal made it possible for all our raw data to be organized and readable. And Larry Hohm did the fine tuning on the software to keep it running smoothly.

Leonard Rifas, cartoonist extraordinaire, composed the cover art.

INTRODUCTION

Time to hit the road again with the new edition of the *Traveler's Guide to Rubber Stamp Stores*. This improved edition is bigger and better (more stores, easier to read, more in each listing). It also maintains all the qualities of the original that stampers have come to know and love (the compact size, maps, discount coupons, and passports). And the *Traveler's Guide* is still the only book that gives detailed information for 100's of stores all across the U.S. and beyond.

STORE LISTINGS

With 550 store listings from almost every state and many Canadian provinces, we have over 120 more stores in this book. There's also more about each store, including whether they sell scrapbook supplies and how many stencils and scissors they carry.

Each listing also covers a wealth of other information about each store. You can find out just about anything—except maybe the owner's birthday. In addition to the store name, address, and phone, we also include:

Store hours

Number of stamps and stamp companies carried

Number of various accessories (stamp pads, markers, papers, books, embossing powders, etc.)

Services offered

Out of state checks and credit cards accepted

To make the stores easy to find, we have listed them alphabetically by state or province, then alphabetically by city, so you can check out store locations at a glance.

MAPS

To make the stores even easier to find, we've included maps for each state and province with a store listed. A dot with the store number shows the general location of each store, so it's easy to know where the stores are anywhere in the state. But we do recommend though that you use a regular street map in addition to this book—most stores do not include our dot and number on their storefronts, so they might otherwise be difficult to locate.

PASSPORT

"Passports" have become popular at rubber stamp shows because rubber stampers collect the colorful designs of various vendors similar to the country stamps on a real passport. We wanted to enable you to add color and to personalize your book.

TRAVELER'S CHEQUE DISCOUNT COUPONS

For your economic enjoyment, we've included eight discount coupons, each good for $1.00 discount on a purchase of $15.00 or more. If you travel enough to use all eight coupons, the book will practically pay for itself—and you'll have a lot more stamps! In addition, the coupons are good clear into the next century (well, OK, that's only a year and a half from publication).

Even if you don't use the coupons, you still might like to look at them to see the Roman woman with the rubber stamp helmet. She was not only designed to look humorous, but she is also endowed with special powers to keep you from getting lost (in case your husband is driving and he can't quite bear to ask directions).

So have a great trip. Send us a postcard and let us know you are having a good time (or that you found new stores we should know about.). Keep in touch.

LISTING LEGEND

[3]Stamps for All Seasons

7833 Chocolate Hwy, Seattle, WA 95008

(206) 329-2677   *M-Th–11-7 F–11-4 Sa–10-6 Su–12-5*

✪ 7,000 ◁ 45 C M S

◻150 ✐250 ▤30 ⊠20 ✪20 ▨30 ✪50 ▥10

C D CA SC N DC   *V M A OSC*

Line 1 Store number on map   Store name

Line 2 Store address

Line 3 Phone   *Hours*

Line 4 ✪ Images ◁ Companies carried C–Custom stamps
M–Make their own line of stamps S–Scrapbook supplies

Line 5* ◻ Stamp pads ✐ Markers ▤ Papers ⊠ Embossing powders ✂ Scissors
▨ Stencils ✪ Stickers ▥ Books, videos & magazines

Line 6 C–Classes D–Demonstrations CA–Customer art displayed SC–Stamp club
HP–House parties N–Newsletter DC–Discount Cards *V–Visa M–Master Card
D–Discover A–American Express OSC–Out of state checks*

*Line 5-Numbers represent *types* or *colors,* total numbers of each accessory is greater.

Apt	Apartment	**Hwy**	Highway	**M**	Monday
Ave	Avenue	**Ln**	Lane	**Tu**	Tuesday
Blvd	Boulevard	**N**	North	**W**	Wednesday
Cswy	Causeway	**S**	South	**Th**	Thursday
Ct	Court	**SC**	Shopping Center	**F**	Friday
Ctr	Center	**Sq**	Square	**Sa**	Saturday
Dr	Drive	**St**	Street	**Su**	Sunday
E	East	**Ste**	Suite		
Expy	Expressway	**Terr**	Terrace	**By appt**	By appointment
Fl	Floor	**Tpke**	Turnpike	**Jan, Feb, etc**	First 3 letters
Fwy	Freeway	**W**	West		of month

ALABAMA

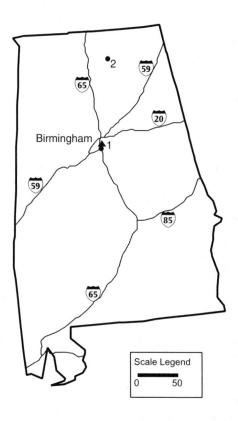

¹Sir Stamps-A-Lot, Inc

186 Oxmoor Rd, Ste A-1, Homewood, AL 35209
(205) 943-9129   *Tu-Sa–10-5*

✪ 2,000 ⊠ 30 M C
  ▭75 ✐200 ▤20 ☗10 ✄7 ▦20 📖10
  C D CA SC DC   *V M OSC*

²The Rubber Stamp Lady, Inc

7914 S Memorial Pkwy, #B-7, Huntsville, AL 35802
(205) 880-1106   *M-F–9:30-6 Sa–9:30-4*

✪ 5,000 ⊠ 40 S
  ▭275+ ✐275+ ▤100 ☗50 ✄10 ▦20 ✪100 📖20
  C D CA SC DC HP   *V M D OSC*

ALASKA

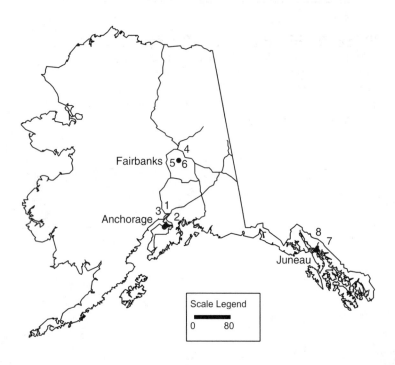

¹Alaska Homecrafters
9900 Old Seward Hwy, Anchorage, AK 99515
(907) 344-7771   M-F–10-8 Sa–10-6 Su–11-5

✪ 1,000 ⊡ 25 C S
  ☐ 50 ✐ 25 ▤ 150 ☖ 75 ✂ 3 ▨ 10 ▭ 10
  C D N DC   V M A D OSC

²Far North Images
510 W 6th Ave, Anchorage, AK 99501
(907) 258-2345   M-Sa–10-6 (Jun-Sep: call)

✪ 30,000 ⊡ 100+ M C S
  ☐ 75 ✐ 275+ ▤ 150 ☖ 50 ✂ 30 ▨ 150+ ✪ 200 ▭ 30
  C D CA N DC HP   V M D

³Joyful Stamp Creations
at Alaska Homecrafters, 9900 Old Seward Hwy, Anchorage, AK 99515
(907) 344-7771   M-Sa–10-8 Su–11-5

✪ 500 ⊡ 15
  ☐ 50 ✐ 25 ▤ 10 ☖ 10 ▨ 10 ▭ 10
  C D   V M

⁴If Only
209 Cushman St, Fairbanks, AK 99701
(907) 457-6659   M-Sa–10-8 (Oct-May: M-Sa–10-6)

✪ 1,000 ⊡ 20 C S
  ☐ 50 ✐ 25 ▤ 50 ☖ 20 ✂ 10 ▨ 150+ ✪ 50 ▭ 3
  C D CA N   V M D

⁵Just For Fun
Regency Ct Mall, Ste 216-2, 59 College Rd, Fairbanks, AK 99701
(907) 452-4386   M-F–11-6 Sa–10-7

S Memory album supplies
  ☐ 25 ✐ 150 ▤ 300+ ☖ 30 ✂ 50 ▨ 100 ✪ 300 ▭ 20
  C D CA N DC HP   V M D OSC

⁶Stamp and Things
Bentley Mall, 32 College Rd, Center Ct, Fairbanks, AK 99701
(907) 455-4386   *M-F–10-9 Sa–10-7 Su–11-6*

✪ 1,000 ▱ 20 C S
   ☐ 50 ✒ 200 📰 100 ⚖ 50 ✂ 10 ✪ 200 📖 10
      C D CA SC N DC HP   *V M D OSC*

⁷Country Charm
2622 John St, Juneau, AK 99801
(907) 364-3529   *By appt*

✪ 500 ▱ 20
   ☐ 50 ✒ 25 📰 30 ⚖ 75 ✂ 10 ✚ 20 📖 3
      C D CA SC N HP   *OSC*

⁸Juneau Rubber Stamp Co
Airport SC, 9131 Glacier Hwy, Juneau, AK 99801
(907) 789-7267   *M-F–10-6*

✪ 3,000 ▱ 15 M C S
   ☐ 75 ✒ 100 📰 30 ⚖ 30 ✂ 30 ✚ 10 ✪ 50 📖 10
      C D CA SC DC   *V M A D*

PASSPORT

ARIZONA

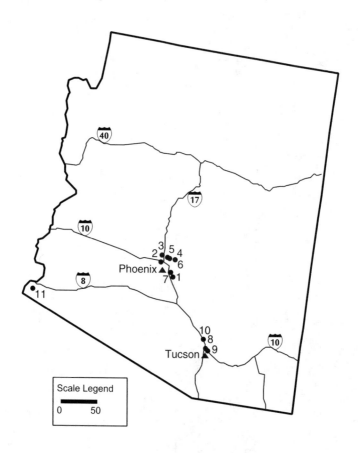

¹Stamp Works
238 S Wall St, Chandler, AZ 85224
(602) 899-5958   *M-Sa–10-5*

☺ 10,000 ☒ 45 M S *Home of copper leaf*
  ☐75 ✏75 ▤30 ▨30 ✄30 ✹20 ☺100 📖25
      C D CA SC N DC   *V M OSC*

STAMP WORKS   hrs. Mon-Sat 10-5

238 S. Wall St.
Chandler, AZ 85224
1-800-579-5958
602-899-5958

over 8000 designs
lots of supplies
great classes   Home of Copper Leaf Creations

²Katie's Closet
7150 N 58th Ave, Glendale, AZ 85301
(602) 937-3750   *M-Sa–10-5*

☺ 10,000 ☒ 90 M S
  ☐200 ▤150 ▨50 ✄30 ✹20 ☺100 📖30
      C D N DC   *V M A D OSC*

³Fascinating Folds
15820 N 35th Ave, #28, Phoenix, AZ 85023
(602) 375-9978   *Tu-F–9-6 Th–9-8 Sa-10-6*

www.fascinating-folds.com
  ▤300+ ✄10 📖70+
      CA   *V M OSC*

⁴Mail Expressions
15260 N Cave Creek Rd, Phoenix, AZ 85032
(602) 971-1003   *M-F–9-5:30 Sa–9-5*

✪ 20,000 ⊠ 100+ M C S
   ⬜200 ✏200 📑100 ⚱50 ✂75+ ⊞100 📖20
   C D CA N DC   ***V M A D***

⁵Stampotique
15440 N 7th St, Ste 17, Phoenix, AZ 85022
(602) 862-0237   *M-F–12-9 Sa–10-5 Su–12-4*

✪ 10,000 ⊠ 100+ S
   ⬜200 ✏275+ 📑200 ⚱100 ✂75+ 📖10
   C D CA SC DC   *V M D OSC*

⁶Crafters Home
Scottsdale Horizon Ctr, 14692 N Frank Lloyd Wright Blvd, #141,
Scottsdale, AZ 85260
(602) 391-3799   *M–9-9 Tu-F–9-7 Sa–9-5*

✪ 10,000 ⊠ 100+ M C S
   ⬜100 ✏275+ 📑250 ⚱100 ✂75+ ⊞150+ ✪3,000+ 📖70+
   C D CA N DC   *V M A D OSC*

⁷Paper Arts Mill & Studio®
930 W 23rd St, Ste 16, Tempe, AZ 85282
(602) 966-1998   *Th-Sa–10-5:30*

S *Stamping & bookbinding papers*
   📑300+ ✂10 📖20
   C D CA   *V M A*

⁸Creative Daze Stamping Arts
522 N 4th Ave, Tucson, AZ 85705
(520) 792-0219   *M-Th–10-6 F,Sa–10-9 Su–12-5*

✪ 500 ⊠ 30 C S
   ⬜75 📑20 ⚱30 ✂3 ⊞10 📖10
   C D CA SC N DC   *V M A D OSC*

⁹Paper Paper Paper
3160 E Fort Lowell Rd, Tucson, AZ 85716
(520) 326-3830   *M-F–10-5:30   Sa–10-4*

✪ 2,000 ⊠ 80 C S *Fabulous papers*
   🗂275+ ✏200 📑300+ ☒150+ ✂20 ▨10 ✿1,000 · 📖30
   C D CA SC N DC   *V M OSC*

¹⁰Papillon Rubber Stamps
Moving-Call for new address, Tucson, AZ 85741
(520) 219-6700

✪ 2,000 ⊠ 10 M C S *Revolving designs, Owners demo*
   🗂150 ✏200 📑200 ☒35 ✂75+ ▨100 📖70+
   C D CA SC N DC HP   *V M A D OSC*

¹¹Stamps Etc
212 Main St, Yuma, AZ 85364
(800) 897-8267   *M-Sa–10-5*

✪ 20,000 ⊠ 100+ C S
   🗂275+ ✏275+ 📑300+ ☒30 ✂20 ▨30 ✿200 📖20
   C D CA N DC   *V M D OSC*

PASSPORT

ARKANSAS

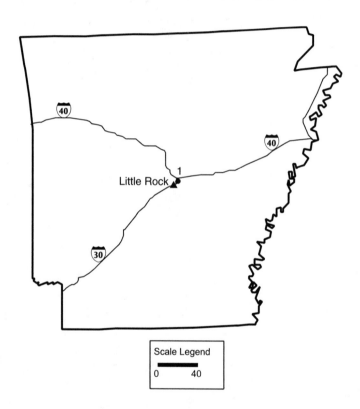

Little Rock

1

Scale Legend

0   40

¹Serendipity Rubber Art Stamps
3812 JFK Blvd, N Little Rock, AR 72116
(501) 758-3453   *Tu-F–10-5 Sa–10-3*

✪ 5,000 ◲ 40 C S
   ▢150 ✐200 ▤100 ▧50 ✂50 ▨50 ✪100 ▭20
   C D CA SC N   *OSC*

CALIFORNIA

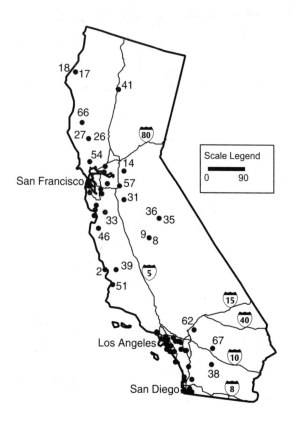

Scale Legend
0   90

San Francisco

Los Angeles

San Diego

SAN FRANCISCO AREA

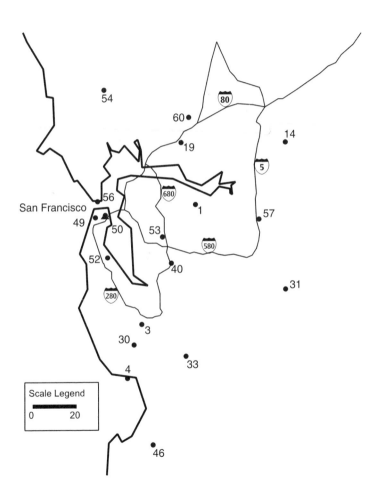

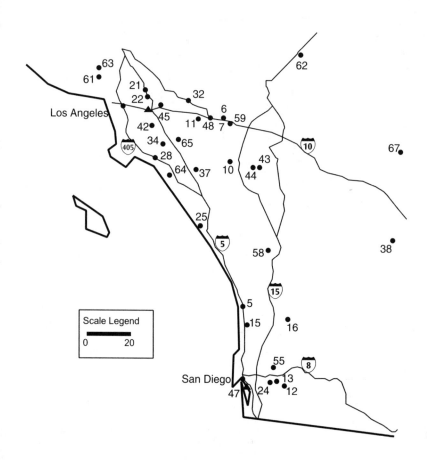

LOS ANGELES AREA

63
61
21
22
32
6
59
Los Angeles
45
11 48 7
42
34
65
405
28
64 37
10
43
44
25
5
58
15
5
15
16
55
8
13
San Diego
24 12
47

62

67

38

Scale Legend

0   20

¹Distinctive Impressions
209 G St, Antioch, CA 94509
(510) 778-3110   *Tu-Sa–10-9:30*

✪ 5,000 ▧ 50 M C S
◻100 ✎200 ▯150 ⌧150+ ✂30 ▨75 ✪50 ▢10
C D CA SC N DC HP   *V M A D OSC*

²Paws On Main Fun Rubber Stamps
816 Main St, Ste C, Cambria, CA 93428
(805) 927-7297   *M-Su–10-5 Closed W*

✪ 10,000 ▧ 100+
◻100 ✎275+ ▯100 ⌧100 ✂10 ✪100 ▢15
D CA   V M D OSC

³The Rubber Stamp Outlet
411 E Campbell Ave, Campbell, CA 95008
(408) 378-2677   *M-Th–11-7 F–11-4 Sa–10-6 Su–12-5*

✪ 8,000 ▧ 45 M S *Paper crafting supplies*
◻150 ✎250 ▯30 ⌧20 ✂20 ✪50
C D CA SC N DC   *V M A OSC*

⁴The Rubber Stamp Lady
1550 41st Ave, Capitola, CA 95010
(408) 479-7981   *M-Sa–10-5*

✪ 15,000 ▧ 100+ M C S
◻75 ✎275+ ▯200 ⌧50 ✂50 ▨20 ✪500 ▢50
C D CA SC N DC   *V M A D*

⁵Gee Gee's Stamps 'N' Stuff
2965 State St, Carlsbad, CA 92008
(760) 729-1779   *M-Sa–10-6 Su–11-4*

✪ 20,000 ▧ 100+ C S
◻150 ✎200 ▯300+ ⌧50 ✂75+ ▨150+ ✪300 ▢50
C D CA SC N DC   *V M A D OSC*

⁶From the Heart

143-A Harvard Ave, Claremont, CA 91711
(909) 626-3479   *M-Sa–10-5:30 F–10-7:30 Su–12-5*

✪ 500 ✉ 15 M S *Over 300 die-cut designs*
    ☐75 ✏275+ ▤300+ ✂75+ ✖100 ✿3,000+ 📖70+
    C D CA N DC   *V M D OSC*

⁷Stamp Your Heart Out

141-C Harvard Ave, Claremont, CA 91711
(909) 621-4363   *M-Sa–10-5:30 F–10-7:30 Su–12-5*

✪ 7,000 ✉ 100+ M C S
    ☐100 ✏200 ▤200 ▧100 ✂75+ ✖20 ✿3,000+ 📖70+
    C D CA N DC   *V M D OSC*

⁸Impressions

10 W Boullard, Ste 101, Clovis, CA 93612
(800) 334-5525   *M-F–10-6 Sa–10-5:30*

✪ 12,000 ✉ 25 C S
    ☐275+ ✏275+ ▤300+ ▧150+ ✂75+ ✖75 ✿3,000+ 📖15
    C D CA SC N DC   *V M A D OSC*

⁹Stamp in the Woods

at Heart's Delight, 457 Pollasky Ave, Old Town Clovis, Clovis, CA 93612
(209) 299-3765   *M-Sa–10-6 Su–11-5*

✪ 1,000 ✉ 5
    ☐25 ✏25 ▤20 ▧20 ✂15 ✖10 ✿50 📖10
    D CA   *V M OSC*

¹⁰SonLight Impressions

125 Business Ctr Dr, Ste E, Corona, CA 91720
(909) 278-5656   *M-F–8-5*

✪ 2,000 ✉ 1 M S
    ☐50 ✏100 ▤30 ▧20 ✂10
                    V M OSC

¹¹Grand Illusions
167 E College St, Covina, CA 91723
(626) 915-7600 *M-F–11-6 Th–11-7 Sa–10-5*

☻ **10,000** ◲ **70 M C S**
◻**250** ✏**275+** ▤**300+** ▨**75** ✂**75+** ▦**150+** ☻**700** ▥**50**
C D CA SC N DC *V M A D OSC*

¹²Stamp Diego
2650 Jamacha Rd, Ste 139, El Cajon, CA 92019
(619) 670-4782 *M-F–9-7 Sa–10-5 Su–12-4*

☻ **20,000** ◲ **100+ C S** *Mail order catalog, $4 refund*
◻**50** ✏**275+** ▤**300+** ▨**30** ✂**50** ▦**150+** ☻**300** ▥**25**
C D CA DC *V M A D OSC*

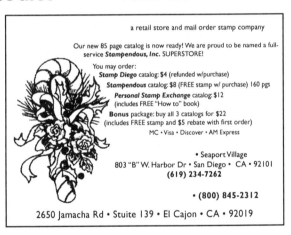

a retail store and mail order stamp company

Our new 85 page catalog is now ready! We are proud to be named a full-service *Stampendous, Inc.* SUPERSTORE!

You may order:
Stamp Diego catalog: **$4** (refunded w/purchase)
Stampendous catalog: **$8** (FREE stamp w/ purchase) 160 pgs
Personal Stamp Exchange catalog: **$12**
(includes FREE "How to" book)
Bonus package: buy all 3 catalogs for **$22**
(includes FREE stamp and $5 rebate with first order)
MC • Visa • Discover • AM Express

• Seaport Village
803 "B" W. Harbor Dr • San Diego • CA • 92101
(619) 234-7262

• **(800) 845-2312**

2650 Jamacha Rd • Stuite 139 • El Cajon • CA • 92019

¹³Stamp Heaven
2284 Fletcher Pkwy, El Cajon, CA 92020
(619) 465-7230 *M-F–10-8 Sa–10-7 Su–12-5*

☻ 20,000 ◲ 100+ C S *Best selection Rubber Moon in US*
◻200 ✏275+ ▤250 ▨75 ✂75+ ▦50 ☻700 ▥50
C D CA SC N DC *V M A D OSC*

¹⁴The Stampers Corner
9633 E Stockton Blvd, Elk Grove, CA 95624
(916) 686-0651   M-F–10-6 Sa–10-5 Su–12-4

✪ 10,000 ☒ 100+ C S
   ☐ 100 ✐ 275+ ▤ 200 ☡ 50 ✂ 50 ▨ 50 ✿ 500 ▥ 30
   C D CA SC N DC   V M A D

¹⁵Gee Gee's Stamps 'N' Stuff
1287 Encinitas Blvd, Encinitas, CA 92024
(760) 634-5770   M-Sa–10-6

✪ 20,000 ☒ 100+ C S
   ☐ 150 ✐ 200 ▤ 300+ ☡ 50 ✂ 75+ ▨ 150+ ✿ 300 ▥ 50
   C D CA SC N DC   V M A D OSC

¹⁶JJ's Stamping Grounds
E Valley Civic Ctr, 2251 E Valley Pkwy, Escondido, CA 92027
(760) 743-6317   M-Th–8:30-5 W,F–8:30-8 Sa–10-4

✪ 12,000 ☒ 100+ C S bboinngg@aol.com
   ☐ 200 ✐ 275+ ▤ 100 ☡ 30 ✂ 75+ ▨ 150+ ✿ 300 ▥ 30
   C D CA SC N DC   V M A OSC

¹⁷Carl Johnson Co
3950 Jacobs Ave, Eureka, CA 95501
(707) 443-4851   M-F–8:30-6 Sa–9-5:30 Su–11-5

✪ 2,000 ☒ 35 S
   ☐ 50 ✐ 150 ▤ 100 ☡ 50 ✂ 50 ▨ 30 ✿ 50 ▥ 25
   C D CA SC N DC HP   V M OSC

¹⁸Eureka Rubber Stamp Co
520 F St, Eureka, CA 95501
(707) 442-0203   M-F–8:30-5:30

✪ 1,000 ☒ 35 M C S
   ☐ 250 ✐ 100 ▤ 50 ☡ 50 ✂ 75+ ▨ 100 ✿ 500 ▥ 3
   D CA SC DC   V M

¹⁹Stamp Heaven
1000 Texas St, Fairfield, CA 94533
(707) 425-6464   *M-Sa–10-5:30 Su–12-4*

✪ 3,000 ☒ 50 S
    ☐275+ ✐275+ ▤150 ☖50 ✂15 ✪100 ▢15
    C D CA SC N DC   *V M A D OSC*

²⁰Your Pad or Mine?
12903 Main St, Garden Grove, CA 92840
(714) 638-4206   ***M–9-5 Tu-Th–9-7 F–9-9 Sa–10-6 Su–10-4***

✪ **5,000** ☒ **100+ C S**
    ☐**200** ✐**200** ▤**150** ☖**50** ✂**75+** ✦**50** ✪**500** ▢**15**
    C D CA SC N HP   ***V M A D OSC***

YOUR PAD OR MINE?

STOP BY & SAY HI AT THE COOLEST
RUBBER STAMP STORE AROUND!
12903 MAIN STREET * GARDEN GROVE *
CALIFORNIA * 92840 * 714-638-4206

²¹Decorative U
1411 Kenneth Rd, Glendale, CA 91201
(818) 246-1790   *Tu-Th–10-6 F,Sa–10-5*

✪ 3,000 ☒ 10 S
    ☐150 ✐275+ ▤100 ☖20 ✂50 ✦150+ ▢10
    C D N   *V M A D OSC*

²²Stamp Stamp Stamp
2172 Glendale Galleria, Glendale, CA 91210
(818) 552-5051   *M–F–10-9 Sa–10-8 Su–11-7*

✪ 12,000 ▱ 60   M C S
   ▭150 ✏275+ ▤50 ♨50 ✂30 ✪100 📖20
   D CA SC DC   *V M A D OSC*

²³Posh Impressions
4708 Barranca Pkwy, Irvine, CA 92603
(949) 651-1145   *M–F–10-8 Sa–10-6 Su–12-5*

✪ 30,000 ▱ 80   M C S
   ▭275+ ✏275+ ▤100 ♨75 ✂75+ ▨50 ✪700 📖50
   C D CA N DC   *V M A OSC*

²⁴Grossmont Opticals/Stamp Delights
8324 Parkway Dr, La Mesa, CA 91942
(619) 465-6873   *M–F–9-6*

✪ 50,000+ ▱ 100+   M C S
   ▭275+ ✏275+ ▤300+ ♨150+ ✂75+ ▨150+ ✪3,000+ 📖70+
   C D CA SC N HP   *V M D OSC*

²⁵Sparkles
23902 Aliso Creek Rd, Laguna Niguel, CA 92677
(949) 362-9211   *M–F–10-7 Sa–10-6 Su–12-5*

✪ 10,000 ▱ 100+   C S
   ▭200 ✏275+ ▤50 ♨50 ✂50 ▨100 ✪700 📖50
   C D CA SC N   *V M A D OSC*

²⁶Shari's Secret Garden
240 N Main St, Lakeport, CA 95453
(707) 263-1647   *M-Sa–10-5:30*

✪ 3,000 ▱ 50   S
   ▭150 ✏275+ ▤300+ ♨50 ✂75+ ▨75 ✪3,000+ 📖25
   C D DC   *V M D OSC*

[27]Stampamania
1045 11th St, Lakeport, CA 95453
(707) 263-0688   M-Sa–10-6

✪ 50,000+ ☒100+ M C S *Rubber stamp paradise at lake*
   ☐275+ ✐150 ▤300+ ♟100 ✂75+ ▨50 ▱70+
   C D CA N DC   *V M OSC*

[28]Stamp Soup
4127 Norse Way, Long Beach, CA 90808
(562) 496-1595   *Tu-Sa–10-5 Every 3rd F–10-8*

✪ 30,000 ☒100+ C S
   ✐250 ▤300+ ♟100 ✂75+ ▨75 ✪200 ▱30
   C D CA SC N DC   *V M A D OSC*

[29]Stamp Stamp Stamp
10250 Santa Monica Blvd, F-134, Los Angeles, CA 90067
(310) 556-3940   *M-F–10-9 Sa–10-6 Su–11-6*

✪ **10,000** ☒**100+ M C S**
   ☐**150** ✐**275+** ▤**50** ♟**50** ✂**30** ✪**100** ▱**15**
   C D CA DC   *V M A D OSC*

[30]The Rubber Stamp Lady
276 N Santa Cruz, Los Gatos, CA 95030
(408) 395-7100   *Tu-Sa–10-5*

✪ 7,000 ☒100+ M C S
   ☐75 ✐275+ ▤50 ♟30 ✂75+ ▨30 ✪50 ▱30
   C D CA N DC   *V M A D*

[31]NASCO Art Supplies
4825 Stoddard Rd, PO Box 3837, Modesto, CA 95352
(209) 529-6957   M-F–8-6 Sa–8-3

✪ 500 ☒1 S *Full line of art supplies*
   ☐25 ✐275+ ▤300+ ♟10 ✂75+ ▨30 ✪100 ▱70+
   C D   *V M A OSC*

³²Stampin' on Cloud 9
403 S Myrtle Ave, Monrovia, CA 91016
(626) 358-2886   *Tu-Sa–11-6 F–11-9*

○ 10,000 ☒ 100+ C S
  ⬜200 ✏250 ▤300+ ☕50 ✂75+ ▦150+ ○3,000+ 📖70+
  C D CA SC N   V M A D

³³The General Store
17390 Monterey Rd, Morgan Hill, CA 95037
(408) 779-9288   *M-F–10-7 Sa–10-6*

○ 15,000 ☒ 60 C S
  ⬜150 ✏250 ▤300+ ☕50 ✂20 ▦150+ ○500 📖3
  C D CA DC   V M

³⁴The Mind's Eye
13560 San Antonio Dr, Norwalk, CA 90650
(562) 863-1714   *M-Sa–11:30-7*

○ 5,000 ☒ 20 S
  ⬜150 ✏75 ▤50 ☕50 ✂15 ▦10 ○500 📖10
  D CA   V M D

³⁵Oakhurst Frameworks and Gifts
49027 Rd 426, PO Box 343, Oakhurst, CA 93644
(209) 683-7845   *M-Sa–10-6 Su–12-5*

○ 5,000 ☒ 20 S
  ⬜200 ✏275+ ▤300+ ☕50 ✂75+ ▦150+ ○3,000+ 📖70+
  D N DC   V M D

³⁶The Cat's Meow
40120 Hwy 41, Ste E, Oakhurst, CA 93644
(209) 642-6611   *Tu-Sa–9-5*

○ 7,000 ☒ 80 C S
  ⬜200 ✏275+ ▤250 ☕75 ✂50 ▦150+ ○200 📖70+
  C D CA N DC   V M A D OSC

37Stamp Fever
320 E Katella, Unit C, Orange, CA 92667
(714) 532-6530   M-F–9-5:30 Sa–Call for hours
✪ 5,000 ✉ 10 M C S
  ☐50 ✐50 📖20 ⚗20 ✂20 ✠10 📖30
  C DC   V M A OSC

38Stamping Grounds
72840 Hwy 111, A-109, Palm Desert, CA 92260
(760) 340-9122   M-F–10-9 Sa–10-7 Su–11-6
✪ 30,000 ✉ 35 C S
  ☐275+ ✐275+ 📖300+ ⚗150+ ✂75+ ✠150+ ✪3,000+ 📖70+
  C D CA SC N DC   V M D OSC

39Stampingly Yours
1220 Park St, Paso Robles, CA 93446
(805) 238-0303   M-F–10-5:30 Sa–10-5
✪ 3,000 ✉ 45 C S
  ☐150 ✐200 📖200 ⚗50 ✂30 ✠75 ✪50 📖25
  C D CA SC N   V M OSC

40California Stampin'
205-D Main St, Pleasanton, CA 94566
(510) 417-8420   M-Sa–10-4 F–10-6
✪ 2,000 ✉ 30 C S *25% off retail mail order*
  ☐50 ✐275+ 📖300+ ⚗50 ✂75+ ✠100 ✪3,000+ 📖70+
  C CA N   V M OSC

41Chestnut's Toys
1127 Hilltop Dr, Redding, CA 96003
(916) 221-8697   M-Sa–10-6
✪ 3,000 ✉ 35 S
  ☐50 ✐200 📖100 ⚗30 ✂30 ✠30 ✪3,000+ 📖10
  C D CA SC N DC   V M A D OSC

⁴²Stamp Stamp Stamp
1815 S Hawthorne, #361, Redondo Beach, CA 90270
(310) 370-3227   M-F–10-9 Sa–10-8 Su–11-7

✪ **12,000** ☒ **50 M C S**
　　☐**150** ✐**275+** ▤**50** ⛾**50** ✂**30** ✪**100** 📖**15**
　　　C D CA SC DC　　　**V M A D OSC**

⁴³Stamp Shack
17120 Van Buren Blvd, Riverside, CA 92504
(909) 780-3050   M-Th–10-6 F–10-7 Sa–10-5 Su–12-4

✪ 3,000 ☒ 35 S
　　☐150 ✐100 ▤300+ ⛾75 ✂30 ▨100 ✪50 📖30
　　　C D CA SC N DC　　　V M OSC

⁴⁴The Stamp Inn
2228 Galleria at Tyler, Riverside, CA 92503
(909) 352-9680   M-F–10-9 Sa–10-7 Su–11-6

✪ 10,000 ☒70 S
　　☐200 ✐275+ ▤250 ⛾100 ✂50 ▨50 ✪500 📖50
　　　D CA N　　　V M D

⁴⁵South Stampadena
1414 El Centro St, S Pasadena, CA 91030
(626) 799-2598   M-F–9:30-6:30 Sa–9:30-2:30

✪ 3,000 ☒20 M C S
　　☐250 ✐275+ ▤50 ⛾50 ✂75+ ▨50 ✪100 📖5
　　　C D CA SC N DC HP   V M A D OSC

⁴⁶Stamp-A-Loons
1024-C S Main St, Salinas, CA 93901
(408) 422-0533   M-Sa–10-5:30 Tu–10-9

✪ 3,000 ☒80 C S
　　☐150 ✐150 ▤100 ⛾50 ✂30 ▨50 ✪50 📖15
　　　C D CA N DC　　　V M A D OSC

⁴⁷Stampaholics™
2802 Juan St, #15, San Diego, CA 92110
(619) 295-3712   M-Sa–10-6 Su–11-5

✪ 12,000 ⊠ 100+ C S
   ☐275+ ✎275+ ▤150 ☖50 ✄75+ ▦150+ ▢25
   C D CA   V M A D OSC

⁴⁸A Stamper's Cottage
145 E Bonita Ave, San Dimas, CA 91773
(909) 305-9990   Tu-Sa–10-5 W–10-8 Su–11-4

✪ 3,000 ⊠ 50 C
   ☐150 ✎200 ▤300+ ☖100 ✄50 ▦50 ▢10
   C D CA SC DC   V M A D OSC

⁴⁹Coco Stamp
Home of Stamp Francisco, 1248 9th Ave, San Francisco, CA 94122
(415) 566-1018   M-Sa–10-6 W–10-9 Su–11-5

✪ **50,000+ ⊠ 100+ M C S**
   ☐275+ ✎275+ ▤300+ ☖150+ ✄75+ ▦150+ ✪1,000 ▢70+
   C D CA DC   V M A

⁵⁰Rubber Stamp Zone
Ghirardelli Sq, 900 N Point St, San Francisco, CA 94109
(415) 929-1539   M-Su–10-6 F,Sa–10-9 (Jun-Sep: M-Su–10-9)

✪ 10,000 ⊠ 35 M S
   ☐200 ✎275+ ▤300+ ☖75 ✄75+ ▦10 ✪500 ▢10
   C D CA SC N DC   V M OSC

⁵¹Stamp Luis Obispo
1036 Chorro St, San Luis Obispo, CA 93401
(805) 541-5198   M-Sa–10-5:30 Th–10-8 Su–11-4

✪ 50,000+ ⊠ 100+ C S
   ☐200 ✎275+ ▤200 ☖100 ✄75+ ▦75 ✪200 ▢30
   C D CA N DC   V M D OSC

[52]Hippo Heart
28 2nd Ave, San Mateo, CA 94401
(650) 347-4477   M-Sa–10-5:30

✪ 20,000 ⊠ 100+ M C S
  ☐ 275+ ✐ 275+ ▥ 250 ▤ 75 ✂ 75+ ▨ 75 ✺ 500 ▭ 50
  C D CA N   V M A D OSC

[53]Stamper's Warehouse
12147 Alcosta Blvd, San Ramon, CA 94583
(925) 833-8764   M-F–11-5:30 Th–10-9 Sa–9:30-5:30 Su–12-5

✪ 12,000 ⊠ 100+ S *Stamp & scrapbook haven*
  ☐ 275+ ✐ 275+ ▥ 300+ ▤ 100 ✂ 75+ ▨ 150+ ✺ 700 ▭ 30
  C D CA SC   V M D OSC

[54]Stampa Rosa
2322 Midway Dr, Santa Rosa, CA 95405
(707) 527-8267   M-Sa–10-6 Su–11-4

✪ 30,000 ⊠ 100+ M C S
  ☐ 275+ ✐ 275+ ▥ 300+ ▤ 150+ ✂ 75+ ▨ 75 ✺ 3,000+ ▭ 50
  C D CA SC DC   V M A D OSC

[55]Stamp La Jolla
10761 Woodside Ave, Ste J, Santee, CA 92071
(619) 449-4600   Th–10-9 F,Sa–10-6

✪ 30,000 ⊠ 100+ M C S
  ☐ 275+ ✐ 275+ ▥ 300+ ▤ 150+ ✂ 75+ ▨ 150+ ✺ 1,000 ▭ 70+
  C D CA N DC   V M D OSC

[56]Rubber Stamp Zone
777 Bridge Way, Sausalito, CA 94965
(415) 331-9601   M-Su–10-6

✪ 10,000 ⊠ 35 M S
  ☐ 200 ✐ 275+ ▥ 300+ ▤ 75 ✂ 75+ ▨ 10 ✺ 500 ▭ 10
  C D CA SC N DC   V M OSC

⁵⁷Ann-ticipations Rubber Stamp Co

6852 Pacific Ave, Ste D, Stockton, CA 95207
(209) 952-5538   M-F–10-6 Th–10-8 Sa–10-4

✪ 7,000 ☒ 40 M C S
   ☐50 ✐275+ 🗐150 ⬗50 ✂30 ⧇100 ✿200 📖15
   C D N   V M D OSC

⁵⁸Murrieta Creek Rubber Stamp Store

28636 Front St, #104, Temecula (Old Town), CA 92590
(909) 694-5534   M-Sa–10-5:30 Su–11-5:30

✪ 3,000 ☒ 35 M C S
   ☐250 ✐275+ 🗐300+ ⬗75 ✂75+ ⧇150+ ✿300 📖20
   C D CA SC N DC   V M A D OSC

⁵⁹Stamping Fools

149 N 2nd Ave, Upland, CA 91786
(909) 931-9140   M-F–10-5:30 Th–12-8:30 Sa–10-5

✪ 7,000 ☒ 100+ C S
   ☐150 ✐75 🗐50 ⬗30 ✂30 ⧇30 ✿50 📖10
   C D CA SC N DC   V M A D OSC

⁶⁰Cowtown Stamp-ede

312-D Cernon St, Vacaville, CA 95688
(707) 446-7256   M-F–10-6 Sa–10-5

✪ 5,000 ☒ 100+ M C S
   ☐150 ✐275+ 🗐300+ ⬗50 ✂50 ⧇75 ✿700 📖20
   C D CA N DC   V M D OSC

⁶¹Stamp Palace

Valencia Town Ctr, 24201 W Valencia Blvd, Ste 2001, Valencia,
CA 91365
(805) 253-1111   M-F–10-9 Sa–10-7 Su–11-6

✪ 7,000 ☒ 100+ C S
   ☐200 ✐275+ 🗐200 ⬗75 ✂75+ ⧇150+ ✿3,000+ 📖50
   C D CA   V M A OSC

⁶²Stamp On In

200-A Walmart Ctr, 15208 Bear Valley Rd, Victorville, CA 92392
(760) 243-0669   Tu-F–10-6 Sa–10-5 Su–12-4

✪ 20,000 ▱ 100 C S
   🗀275+ ✏275+ 📕300+ 🗏150+ ✂75+ ✐100 📖70+
   C D CA SC N DC   V M D OSC

⁶³West Hills Rubber Stamp Shoppe

8230 Fallbrook Ave, W Hills, CA 91304
(818) 710-1551   Tu-F–10-7 Sa–10-4 Su–12-5

✪ 7,000 ▱ 100+ C S
   🗀275+ ✏275+ 📕300+ 🗏150+ ✂75+ ✐150+ ✪1,000 📖70+
   C D CA SC N DC   V M A OSC

⁶⁴Stamp-A-DoodleDo!

16418 Beach Blvd, Westminster, CA 92683
(714) 848-4800   M-F–10-8:30 Tu,W,Sa–10-6 Su–11-4:30

✪ 20,000 ▱ 100+ C S
   🗀275+ ✏275+ 📕300+ 🗏100 ✂75+ ✐200 ✪700 📖125
   C D CA SC N DC   V M A D

⁶⁵Stampin' Pad

16248 Whittier Blvd, Whittier, CA 90603
(562) 902-9692   M-F–10-6 Sa–10-5

✪ 12,000 ▱ 90 C S
   🗀100 ✏250 📕100 🗏30 ✂20 ✐20 ✪1,000 📖15
   C D CA SC N DC   V M OSC

⁶⁶The Goods' Stamp Shoppe

56 S Main, Willits, CA 95490
(707) 459-1363   M-Th–10-5:30 F,Sa–10-9 Su–12-4

✪ 7,000 ▱ 60 M C S
   🗀275+ ✏275+ 📕300+ 🗏150+ ✂75+ ✐50 ✪1,000 📖12
   C D CA N   V M A D OSC

⁶⁷The Stamp Stop
55831 29 Palms Hwy, Yucca Valley, CA 92284
(760) 228-5021   *Tu-Sa–10-5*

✪ 2,000 ▱ 15 S

   ☐ 100 ✎ 150 ▤ 275 ♟ 100 ✂ 75+ ▨ 150+ ✪ 1,000 ▥ 30
   C D CA N DC   *OSC*

PASSPORT

COLORADO

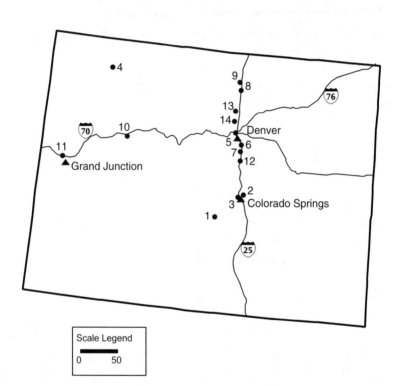

¹Stamp of Excellence Inc
1105 Main St, Cañon City, CO 81212
(719) 275-8422   M-Th–8:30-5:15 W,F–10-5:15

✪ 2,000 ✉ 5 M C S *Line of Christian stamps*
▢200 ✐70 ▤100 ☕30 ✄75+ ▨30 ▥10
C D CA DC HP   V M A D OSC

²Creative Impressions
2520 W Colorado Ave, Colorado Springs, CO 80904
(719) 577-4858   M-Sa–10-6 Su–12-5

✪ 15,000 ✉ 100+ M C S
▢200 ✐275+ ▤300+ ☕150+ ✄75+ ▨150+ ✪500 ▥70+
C D N DC   V M D OSC

³Simple Pleasures
2833 Dublin Blvd, Colorado Springs, CO 80918
(719) 528-1338   M-Sa–9:30-5:30 Th–9:30-8

✪ 30,000 ✉ 100+ C S
▢150 ✐275+ ▤300+ ☕100 ✄50 ▨150+ ✪1,000 ▥70+
C D CA N DC   V M D OSC

⁴Jackson's Office Supply
106 W Victory Way, Craig, CO 81625
(970) 824-8114   M-Sa–8-5:30

✪ 3,000 ✉ 15 C S
▢150 ✐250 ▤300+ ☕100 ✄15 ▨50 ✪300 ▥30
C D CA SC DC   V M A D

⁵About Memories
1557 W 84th Ave, Ste G, Denver, CO 80221
(303) 233-1860   M–12-9 Tu-F–10-9 Sa–10-5 Su–1-4

✪ 2,000 ✉ 25 C S
▢100 ✐100 ▤300+ ☕75 ✄50 ▨30 ✪500 ▥30
C D CA SC N DC   V M D OSC

⁶The Happy Stamper
2703 E 3rd Ave, Denver, CO 80206
(303) 322-2489   M-Sa–10-6 Su–11-5

✪ 20,000 ⊠ 40 M C S
  ☐250 ✏275+ ▤150 ⚖30 ✂75+ ▦100 ✪3,000+ ▢20
  C D CA SC N DC   **V M A D OSC**

⁷Paper Wares
7475 E Arapahoe Rd, Englewood, CO 80112
(303) 850-0520   M-F–9-6 Sa–9-5 Su–11-3

✪ 5,000 ⊠ 70 C S
  ☐275+ ✏275+ ▤300+ ⚖150+ ✂75+ ▦30 ✪300 ▢25
  C D CA N DC   **V M A OSC**

⁸Stamp World
Foothills Fashion Mall, 215 E Foothills Pkwy, Ft Collins, CO 80525
(970) 282-9591   M-Su–10-9

✪ 12,000 ⊠ 50 C S
  ☐275+ ✏275+ ▤100 ⚖30 ✂20 ▦50 ✪500 ▢15
  C D CA SC N DC   **V M A D OSC**

⁹Uptown Rubber Stamps
132 W Mountain Ave, Ft Collins, CO 80524
(970) 493-3212   M-F–10-6 Sa–10-5 Su–12-4

✪ 12,000 ⊠ 100+ M C S *Uptown stamps,Unmounted rubber*
  ☐275+ ✏275+ ▤300+ ⚖150+ ✂50 ✪700 ▢25
  C D CA SC N DC   **V M D OSC**

¹⁰Andréa Stamps, Ink
720 Grand Ave, Glenwood Springs, CO 81601
(970) 945-5088   M-Th–10-5:30 Tu,F–10-8 Sa–10-5 Su–10-7

✪ 2,000 ⊠ 35 C S
  ☐275+ ✏250 ▤200 ⚖75 ✂20 ▦10 ✪100 ▢15
  C D CA N DC   **V M D OSC**

¹¹Crafters Home

Mesa Mall, 2424 Hwy 6 & 50, #510, Grand Junction, CO 81505
(800) 486-3534   *M-Sa–10-9 Su–11-6*

✪ 10,000 ⊠ 100+ M C S

⬜100 ✐275+ 📰250 ⧗100 ✄75+ ✠150+ ✪3,000+ 📖70+
C D CA N DC   V M D

¹²Stamp World

Southglenn Mall, 6911 University Blvd, Littleton, CO 80122
(303) 734-0800   *M-Su–10-9*

✪ 12,000 ⊠ 50 C S

⬜200 ✐275+ 📰100 ⧗30 ✄20 ✠150+ ✪500 📖15
C D CA SC N DC   V M A D OSC

¹³The Pampered Stamper Etc

721 9th Ave, Longmont, CO 80501
(303) 682-1223   *M-Sa–10-5*

✪ 7,000 ⊠ 50 C S

⬜75 ✐250 📰50 ⧗20 ✄75+ ✠100 ✪50 📖5
C D CA DC   V M A D OSC

¹⁴Stamp World

Westminster Mall, 5471 W 88th Ave, Westminster, CO 80030
(303) 427-7143   *M-Su–10-9*

✪ 12,000 ⊠ 50 C S

⬜200 ✐275+ 📰100 ⧗30 ✄20 ✠150+ ✪500 📖15
C D CA SC N DC   V M A D OSC

PASSPORT

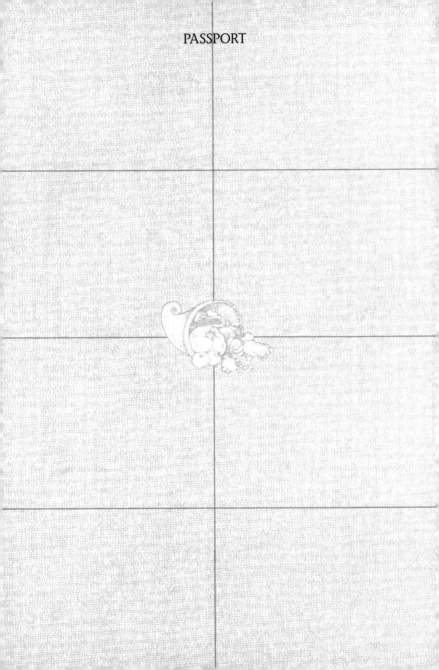

CONNECTICUT

Hartford

New Haven

¹Lasting Impressions
198 Greenwood Ave, Bethel, CT 06801
(203) 792-3740   *M-F–10-6 Sa–10-5*

✪ 2,000 ◫ 20 M C
　　◻75 ✐50 ▤30 ☒10 ✂20 ▦20 ▢15
　　CA SC   *V M D OSC*

²Shoreline Stamp Shoppe
188 N Main St, Rte 1, Branford, CT 06405
(203) 488-9464   *M-Sa–10-5 Su–10-4*

✪ 15,000 ◫ 100+ C S
　　◻275+ ✐275+ ▤200 ☒150+ ✂75+ ▦100 ✪1,000 ▢70+
　　C D CA SC N DC HP   *V M D OSC*

³Impressive Impressions
1027 Farmington Ave, Farmington, CT 06032
(860) 676-8601   *M-Sa–10-5 Th–10-8 Su–12-5*

✪ 12,000 ◫ 100+ C S
　　◻150 ✐275+ ▤100 ☒75 ✂50 ▦100 ✪50 ▢20
　　C D CA N DC   *V M A D OSC*

⁴Salon de Stampe: An Inspiration Resource
16 Lewis St, Greenwich, CT 06830
(203) 552-0080   *M-Sa–10:00-5:30*

✪ 7,000 ◫ 80 C S *Custom special events*
　　◻275+ ✐275+ ▤300+ ☒150+ ✂75+ ▦150+ ✪200 ▢70+
　　C D CA N DC   *V M A OSC*

⁵Country Impressions
3 Maple St, Kent, CT 06757
(860) 927-1717   *M-Sa–10-5:30 Su–12-5*

✪ 1,000 ◫ 15 C S
　　◻100 ✐250 ▤200 ☒30 ✂20 ▦50 ▢25
　　C D CA SC N DC HP   *V M D OSC*

⁶Love At First Stamp
4 Albatross Dr, Ledyard, CT 06339
(860) 572-0596   M–9-12 W–9-12, 1-4 Th–6:30-10 F–1-4 Sa–9-12

✪ 5,000 ⊠ 100+ S
　□75 ✐200 ▤100 ☷50 ✂30 ▓10 ▭10
　C D CA SC N DC HP   OSC

⁷Finally Woolies
78 N Moodus Rd, Moodus, CT 06469
(860) 873-1111   Tu-Sa–10-5:30 Th–10-7

✪ 1,000 ⊠ 30 C
　□50 ✐75 ▤50 ☷20 ✂3 ▭5
　C D CA N   V M D OSC

⁸The Village Stitchery
Olde Mistick Village, Mystic, CT 06355
(860) 536-0424   M-Sa–10-6 (Jun-Aug: 10-8) Su–12-5

✪ 5,000 ⊠ 50 S
　□100 ✐75 ▤100 ☷50 ✂30 ▓75 ✪50 ▭30
　C D CA SC N DC   V M A D

⁹Stamps & Such
1 Sachem Terr, Norwich, CT 06360
(860) 887-4535   W–7-9 pm +by appt

✪ 2,000 ⊠ 25 S Scrapbook supplies & classes
　□100 ✐50 ▤200 ☷50 ✂10 ▭15
　C D CA SC N DC HP   V M D OSC

¹⁰The Stampers' Cove
Riverbend Plz, 1079 Queen St (Rte 10), Southington, CT 06689
(860) 747-2087   Tu-Sa–10-5 Th–10-8 Su–12-5

✪ **10,000** ⊠ **100** **S**
　□**200** ✐**250** ▤**300+** ☷**100** ✂**30** ▓**50** ✪**50** ▭**50**
　C D CA N   V M A D OSC

Impressive Impressions is
New England's #1
Art Rubberstamp & Memory Album Store!

As you travel to and from New England you pass right by our store - a few minutes west of Hartford - just off Exit 39 on I 84 and minutes from I-91. We are 1.8 miles on the left after the light at the end of the exit. Directly opposite a golf driving range. Impressive Impressions started over six years ago in Farmington, CT and has grown to be the largest number one resource center for all your stamping and memory album needs. We have thousands of stamps, supplies and samples from over 120 companies along with our exclusive memory album department stocked with all the latest acid-free papers, templates, stickers, albums and hundreds of supplies for you to create that special memory album. Plus we have our new arrival section to showcase all the latest stamps and products.

Impressive Impressions also has a friendly, talented, knowledgeable and very versatile staff that has many years of stamping experience. We offer classes from beginning to advanced stamping, teaching the latest techniques in stamping, scrapbooking, calligraphy and all new products that are on the cutting edge in the industry. We love to demonstrate all levels of stamping and as always we are the first to show you the latest and greatest from the rubberstamping world. Our goal is to make you a successful rubberstamp artist!

Please come and visit us to add another wonderful experience to your rubberstamping journey!

Location:	Hours:
1027 Farmington Ave.	**7 days a week**
Farmington, CT 06032	**Mon, Tues, Wed, Fri. 10-5;**
860-676-8601	**Thurs. 10-8;**
	Sat. 10-5; Sun. 12-5

¹¹The Stamp'n Grounds at Kathy Johns
at Kathy Johns, Rtes 195 & 44, Storrs, CT 06268
(860) 429-0362   *M-Su–10-11*

✪ 10,000 ⬚ 90
　　⬚250 ✐275+ ▤200 ▦150+ ✄20 ✪100 📖20
　　C   OSC

¹²The Stamp Corner
327 N Colony Rd, Rte 5, Wallingford, CT 06492
(203) 269-6662   *Tu-F–10-5 Sa–10-4*

✪ 1,000 ⬚ 20 M C
　　⬚50 ✐150 ▤75 ▦50 ✖30 📖25
　　C D CA N   ***V M OSC***

¹³Great American Stamp Store
1015 Post Rd E, Westport, CT 06880
(203) 221-1229   *M-F–10-6 Th–10-8 Sa–10-5 Su–12-5*

✪ 12,000 ⬚ 100+ M C S
　　⬚200 ✐200 ▤200 ▦50 ✄75+ ✖100 ✪100 📖70+
　　C D CA N   V M OSC

¹⁴Stampressions, LLC
Rear of Corner Book Store, Shops at Ledgebrook, Rte 44, Winsted,
CT 06098
(860) 738-0338   *M-W–10-6 Th,F–10-8 Sa–10-5 Su–11-4*

✪ 10,000 ⬚70 C S
　　⬚100 ✐250 ▤100 ▦50 ✄15 ✖50 📖10
　　C D CA SC N DC   V M OSC

FLORIDA

Jacksonville

13

21

22

Orlando

3

5

6

9

Tampa

24

1   2

18

20

Fort Myers

19   4   12

16

23

7

17

Scale Legend

0   60

8

EASTERN FLORIDA

¹Keeton's Office & Art Supply

817 Manatee Ave W, Bradenton, FL 34205
(941) 747-2995   M-F–8:30-5

✪ 2,000 ◁ 15 C S
  ▢275+ ✏275+ ▤150 ▨30 ✄30 ▦10 ▥15
  D CA N DC   V M D OSC

²Mother & Child

6709 Manatee Ave W, Bradenton, FL 34209
(941) 792-9416   M-F–10-5 Sa–10-3

✪ 1,000 ◁ 25
  ▢75 ✏150 ▤300+ ▨75 ✄50 ✪700 ▥70+
  C D CA SC   V M

³North Star Bear and Stamp Store

1126 W Jefferson St, Brooksville, FL 34601
(352) 796-8970   Tu-Sa–10-5

✪ 5,000 ◁ 20
  ▢200 ✏25 ▤100 ▨75 ✄20 ▦75 ▥10
  D CA   V M D OSC

⁴Rubber Dub Dub, Inc

2816 Del Prado Blvd, #3, Cape Coral, FL 33904
(941) 540-4141   M-Sa–10-6 +(Jan-Apr: Su–12-5)

✪ **20,000 ◁ 100+ M C S Unmounted with foam backings**
  ▢275+ ✏275+ ▤100 ▨50 ✄75+ ▦100 ✪50 ▥15
  C D CA SC N DC   V M D OSC

⁵Planet Rubber

2620 State Rd 590, Clearwater, FL 34619
(813) 669-4114   Tu-Sa–10-5

✪ 10,000 ◁ 40 M S
  ▢75 ✏275+ ▤150 ▨50 ✄75+ ▦30 ✪200 ▥50
  C D CA N DC   V M D OSC

⁶Azalea Hill
13 S Blvd, PO Drawer 1594, (Zip) 33836, Davenport, FL 33837
(941) 422-8070   *Tu-F–10-4*

✪ 5,000 ▱ 10 C
　　▱50 ✎100 ▯50 ☕50 ✂20 🖼100 📖20
　　C D CA SC N DC   *V M OSC*

⁷Wonderland Emporium
3055 S Federal Hwy, Delray Beach, FL 33483
(561) 276-7116   *M-F–10-6 Sa–10-5 +(Sep-Apr: Su–12-4)*

✪ **20,000 ▱ 100+ M C S**
　　▱150 ✎200 ▯250 ☕100 ✂75+ 🖼20 ✿200 📖15
　　C D CA N DC   *V M A D OSC*

⁸Artstamps of Key West
507 Southward St, Key West, FL 33040
(305) 296-2201   *M-Sa–10-6*

✪ 1,000 ▱ 25
　　▱100 ✎200 ▯30 ☕20 ✂5 📖5
　　C D CA DC HP   *V M A D OSC*

⁹Gone Stampin'
5131 S Florida Ave, Ste #6, Lakeland, FL 33813
(941) 647-9562   *Tu-F–10-5:30 Sa–10-5*

✪ **10,000 ▱ 70 C S**
　　▱75 ✎250 ▯200 ☕150+ ✂15 🖼30 ✿500 📖10
　　C D CA N DC   *V M OSC*

¹⁰Stamp Your Art Out
127 E Hwy 434, Longwood, FL 32750
(407) 830-8865   *Tu-F–10-6 Sa–10-3*

✪ **50,000+ ▱ 100+ C S *Largest selection anywhere***
　　▱275+ ✎275+ ▯300+ ☕150+ ✂75+ 🖼150+ ✿3,000+ 📖70+
　　C D CA SC DC   *V M A D*

¹¹Stamp Cabana
Merritt Sq Mall, 777 E Merritt Island Cswy, Merritt Island, FL 32952
(407) 454-7747   *M-Sa–10-9 Su–12-5*

✪ 50,000+ ⊠100+ M C S
☐275+ ✐275+ ▤300+ ⚱150+ ✄75+ ▨150+ ✪3,000+ ▥70+
C D CA N DC   *V M A D*

¹²G & G Artistic Stamps
2316 Kirkwood Ave, Naples, FL 34110
(941) 774-2431   *M-F–8-5 Sa–8-12*

✪ 7,000 ⊠60
☐50 ✐100 ▤50 ⚱150+ ✄50 ▨30 ▥3
C D CA N DC   *V M A D OSC*

¹³A Small Cleverness
868 Blanding Blvd, Ste 113, Orange Park, FL 32065
(904) 272-0503   *M-F–10-6 Sa–10-5*

✪ 5,000 ⊠100+ C S
☐100 ✐275+ ▤100 ⚱50 ✄50 ▨75 ✪50 ▥20
C D CA SC   *V M A D OSC*

¹⁴Stamp Cabana

5428 Touchstone Dr, Orlando, FL 32819
(407) 363-5530   *M-Sa–10-9 Su–12-5*

✪ 50,000+ ▱ 100+ M C S
   ▱275+ ✐275+ ▤300+ ▨150+ ✂75+ ▨150+ ✪3,000+ ▱70+
   C D CA N DC   *V M A D*

¹⁵Stamp Your Art Out

9225 S Orange Blossom Trail, Orlando, FL 32837
(407) 816-0037   *Tu-F–10-6 Sa–10-3*

✪ **50,000+ ▱ 100+ C S *Largest selection anywhere***
   ▱**275+** ✐**275+** ▤**300+** ▨**150+** ✂**75+** ▨**150+** ✪**3,000+** ▱**70+**
   C D CA SC DC   ***V M A D***

¹⁶D's Rubber Stamps

2900 W Sample Rd, #1323, Pompano Beach, FL 33073
(954) 975-5975   *Tu-F–9:30-5 Sa,Su–9:30-6*

✪ 5,000 ▱ 20 C S
   ▱50 ✐100 ▤30 ▨20 ✂30 ▨10 ▱5
   D CA   *A*

¹⁷The Paper Garden
2765 E Atlantic Blvd, Pompano Beach, FL 33062
(954) 942-7699   M-Sa–10-6 +by appt

✪ 3,000 ⊡ 25 M C
⬜75 ✎75 ▤30 ♨30 ✂10 ▦10 ✪100 📖5
C D SC N   V M A

¹⁸Rubber Stamp Artists' Camp
3805-B Tamiani Trl, Port Charlotte, FL 33952
(941) 743-9622   W-Sa–10-5 Tu–10-8

✪ 2,000 ⊡ 20 C
⬜75 ✎75 ▤50 ♨50 ✂50 ▦50 📖20
C   V M D OSC

¹⁹Three Crafty Ladies
1620 Periwinkle Way, Sanibel, FL 33957
(941) 472-2893   M-Su–9:30-5 (Apr-Oct: Closed Su)

✪ 12,000 ⊡ 20 S
⬜100 ✎200 ▤50 ♨50 ✂15 ▦50 ✪50 📖5
D   V M D OSC

²⁰Sarasota Stamps
4245 Bee Ridge Rd, Sarasota, FL 34233
(941) 378-4673   Tu-F–10-6 Sa–10-5

✪ 7,000 ⊡ 20 M C S
⬜75 ✎275+ ▤150 ♨30 ✂30 ✪100 📖20
C D CA N DC   V M D OSC

²¹Claire's Collectibles
78-B San Marco Ave, St Augustine, FL 32084
(904) 825-1122   M-Sa–10-5 Su–12-5

✪ 12,000 ⊡ 100+ C S
⬜200 ✎200 ▤100 ♨150+ ✂75+ ▦30 ✪200 📖25
C D CA N DC HP   V M A OSC

²²Stamp Augustine

11-A Aviles St, St Augustine, FL 32084
(904) 829-1560   *M-Su–10-5 Closed Th*

✪ 10,000 ▱ 70
☐200 ✐200 ▤100 ⬓20 ✄10 ▱20
C D CA DC   *V M OSC*

²³Inkredible! Stamp Art

910 S Dixie Hwy, Stuart, FL 34994
(561) 287-2294   *M-F–8-5:30*

✪ 2,000 ▱ 20 C
☐200 ✐150 ▤50 ⬓20 ✄10 ▨50 ✪3,000+ ▱15
CA SC DC   *V M A D OSC*

²⁴Tamp-A-Stamp

2219 S Dale Mabry Hwy, Tampa, FL 33629
(813) 258-8682   *M-F–9-5 Sa–10-5*

✪ 5,000 ▱ 50 M C S
☐275+ ✐275+ ▤300+ ⬓150+ ✄75+ ▨150+ ✪700 ▱70+
C D CA SC N DC HP   *V M A D OSC*

²⁵Stamp Cabana Winter Park

352 Park Ave S, Winter Park, FL 32789
(407) 628-8863   *M-Sa–10-9 Su–12-5*

✪ 50,000+ ▱ 100+ M C S
☐275+ ✐275+ ▤300+ ⬓150+ ✄75+ ▨150+ ✪3,000+ ▱70+
C D CA N DC   *V M A D*

GEORGIA

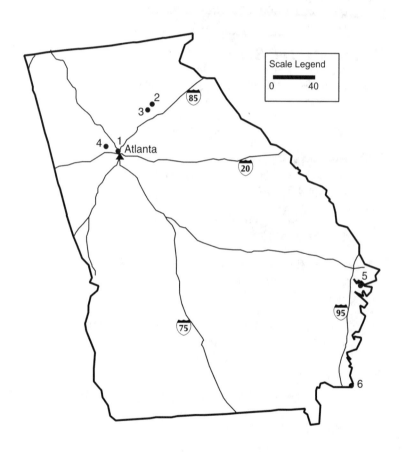

¹Ichiyo Art Center, Inc
432 E Paces Ferry Rd, Atlanta, GA 30305
(404) 233-1846   M-Sa–10-6

✪ 1,000 ▱ 5 M C *Asian images, Japanese papers*
  🗐300+ 📖10
    C CA   *V M A D OSC*

²Stampworks
110 Bradford St NW, Gainesville, GA 30501
(770) 531-9692   M,Tu,F–10-5 Th–10-7 Sa–10-4 +by appt

✪ **10,000 ▱ 50 C S *Scrapbooking, Invitations***
  ▢150 ✐200 🗐200 ⚱75 ✂50 ▨100 ✪500 📖20
    C D CA N DC   *V M D OSC*

³The Stamper's Pad
350 Shallowford Rd, Gainesville, GA 30504
(770) 532-0370   M-F–10-5 Sa–10-4

✪ 10,000 ▱ 30 C S
  ▢50 ✐50 🗐20 ⚱20 ✂20 📖5
    C D CA N DC   *V M OSC*

⁴Rubber Stamp Fantasy
136 S Park Sq, Marietta, GA 30060
(770) 590-8500   M-Sa–11-7

✪ 12,000 ▱ 60 M C S
  ▢275+ ✐275+ 🗐250 ⚱100 ✂20 ▨100 📖20
    C D CA N DC   *V M OSC*

⁵Savannah Impressions
at Colonial Quilts, 11710 Largo Dr, Savannah, GA 31419
(912) 925-0055   M-Sa–10-6

✪ 500 ▱ 1 M S
  ▢50 ✐100 🗐300+ ⚱10 ✂30 ▨30 ✪100 📖10
    C D N DC   *V M A D*

⁶Old Town Crafts

101 E Weed St, St Marys, GA 31558
(912) 882-9000   *M-Su–10-5*

✪ 5,000 ⊡ 45 M C S
   ☐50 ✐275+ ▤150 ⬚75 ✂15 ✻10 ✪50 📖10
   C D CA SC N DC HP   *V M A D OSC*

PASSPORT

HAWAII

4 1
2 3
Honolulu

Scale Legend

0   30

¹Munchkins
98-029 Hekaha St, #16, Aiea, HI 96701
(808) 488-7867   *M-F–10-5 W–10-6 Sa–10-4 Su–10-2*

✪ 3,000 ▨ 60 C S
    ☐100 ✐275+ ▤50 ⚱150+ ✂15 ▩20 ✪50 ⬚15
    C D CA N DC   *V M A D OSC*

²Cute Stuff
Puck's Alley, 2600 S King St, #204, Honolulu, HI 96826
(808) 944-2097   *M-F–10-6 Sa–9-6 Su–10-4*

✪ 5,000 ▨ 50 C S
    ☐75 ✐200 ▤50 ⚱30 ✂20 ⬚25
    C D CA N DC   *V M*

³Taj Clubhouse
Ward Warehouse, 1050 Ala Moana Blvd, #A-7, Honolulu, HI 96814
(808) 947-3788   *M-Sa–10-9 Su–10-5*

✪ 1,000 ▨ 1 M S
    ☐50 ✐275+ ▤50 ⚱50 ✂30 ▩75 ✪1,000 ⬚15
    C D CA SC N DC   *V M A D OSC*

⁴The Funnery
94-340 Ukee St, #4, Waipahu, HI 96797
(808) 677-7852   *Tu-F–9-7 (closed 1-2:45) Sa–9-7 Su–10-5*

✪ 1,000 ▨ 100+ C S
    ☐100 ✐150 ▤150 ⚱100 ✂5 ✪50 ⬚15
    C D CA N DC   *V M OSC*

IDAHO

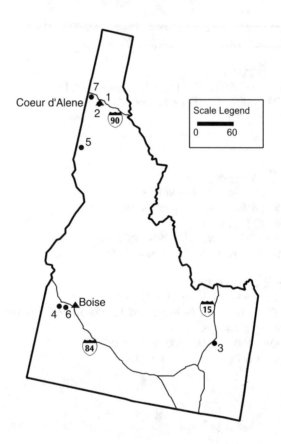

¹Bear Springs Crafts/Bear Rubber
1928 N 4th St, Coeur d'Alene, ID 83814
(208) 666-9115   *M-Su–10-6*

✪ 7,000 ▱ 50 M S
◻150 ✐200 ▤200 ☕50 ✂20 ▨50 ✪200 📖25
C D CA SC N DC   *V M D OSC*

²Rubber Addicts dba NW Business Stamps
207 Sherman Ave, Coeur d'Alene, ID 83814
(208) 769-7354   *M-Sa–10-6*

✪ 2,000 ▱ 1 M C S
◻75 ✐100 ▤100 ☕50 ✂20 ▨20 📖25
C D CA SC N DC   *V M A D OSC*

³Park Avenue Stamps
310 Park Ave, Idaho Falls, ID 83402
(208) 525-2560   *Tu-F–10-6 Sa–10-4*

✪ 5,000 ▱ 25 M C S
◻100 ✐150 ▤100 ☕50 ✂50 📖5
C D CA SC N DC   *V M D*

⁴Stamp Station
1326 E 1st St, Meridian, ID 83642
(208) 884-4002   *Tu-Sa–10-6 M,Th–10-8 Su–12-5*

✪ 3,000 ▱ 90 C S
◻275+ ✐275+ ▤100 ☕75 ✂75+ ▨100 ✪50 📖30
C D CA SC N DC   *V M D OSC*

⁵Stampin' From the Heart
3609 Reams Rd, Moscow, ID 83843
(888) 882-6158   *Call for hours*

✪ 2,000 ▱ 25 C S
◻100 ✐75 ▤100 ☕50 ✂30 ▨50 📖30
C D CA SC N DC HP   *V M OSC*

⁶Stampin FUNaddict
203 6th Ave S, #2, Nampa, ID 83651
(208) 465-0500   M–10-8 Tu-Sa–10-6

✪ 2,000 ▱70 M C S
  ▭75 ✎150 🗐150 ⧗50 ✁30 ❊75 📖25
  C D CA N DC   V M D OSC

⁷Stampa Doodle Doo
3825 N Chase Rd, Post Falls, ID 83854
(208) 773-9498   Tu-F–11-5:30 Th–11-8 Sa–10-5

✪ 3,000 ▱40
  ▭75 ✎100 🗐300+ ⧗30 ✁30 ❊20 📖10
  C D CA DC   V M D OSC

PASSPORT

ILLINOIS

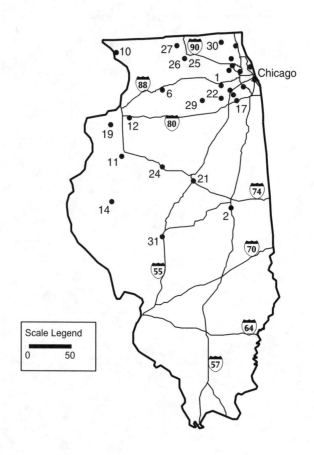

NORTHERN ILLINOIS

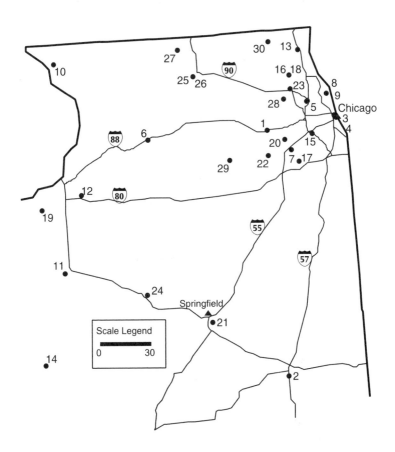

¹The Stamper's Corner
3 S Batavia Ave, Batavia, IL 60510
(630) 406-8642   *Tu-F–11-5 Th–11-7 Sa–10-5 Su–12-3*

✪ 10,000 ⊠ 100+ C S

☐100 ✐100 ▤300+ ▨75 ✂75+ ▨150+ ✪1,000 📖25
C D CA SC N DC   *V M A OSC*

²Prairie Gardens, Inc
3000 W Springfield, Champaign, IL 61821
(217) 356-6532   *M-F–9-9 Sa–8-6 Su–10-5*

✪ 1,000 ⊠ 5 S
☐50 ✐100 ▤300+ ▨20 ✂50 ▨50 ✪500 📖20
C D CA SC N   *V M D OSC*

³Paper Source
232 W Chicago Ave, Chicago, IL 60610
(312) 337-0798   *M-F–10-6:30 Sa–10-5 Su–12-5*

✪ 3,000 ⊠ 100+ M C S *1000's of papers, Kool stuff*
☐200 ✐150 ▤300+ ▨50 ✂40 ▨20 ✪40 📖50
C D CA SC N   *V M A D OSC*

⁴Stamp-O-Rama at Brooks
55 E Washington (at Wabash), Chicago, IL 60602
(312) 372-2504   *M-F–8-6 Sa–9-4*

✪ 2,000 ⊠ 15 M *Kitsch/Vintage/Cool Stamps*
☐25 ✂10 📖10
CA   *V M A D OSC*

⁵Carolina Moon
River Bend Plz, 1952 River Rd, Des Plaines, IL 60018
(847) 297-9622   *M-Sa–10-6 Tu,Th–10-8*

✪ 12,000 ⊠ 50 C S *Pencil imprinting, Lamination*
☐100 ✐100 ▤300+ ▨100 ✂75+ ▨75 ✪200 📖25
C D CA SC N DC   *V OSC*

⁶Baskets & More
81 S Hennepin Ave, Dixon, IL 61021
(815) 288-7337   M-F–9-5:30 Sa–9-5 +(Sep-Jun: Su–12-1)

✪ 30,000 ▱ 50 S
⬜275+ ✐200 ▤150 ⚱75 ✂20 ▨75 ▥10
D DC   V M D OSC

⁷Rubber Side Down
5232 Main St, Downers Grove, IL 60440
(630) 241-9928   Tu-F–11-6 Th–11-8 Sa–10-5 Su–12-4

✪ 10,000 ▱ 50 C S
⬜150 ✐275+ ▤200 ⚱100 ✂10 ▨30 ✪700 ▥70+
C D CA SC N DC HP   V M D OSC

⁸Paper Source
2112 Central St, Evanston, IL 60201
(847) 733-8830   M-F–10-6:30 Sa–10-5 Su–12-4

✪ 1,000 ▱ 100+ M C S 1000's of paper, Kool stuff
⬜200 ✐150 ▤300+ ⚱50 ✂40 ▨20 ✪40 ▥50
C D CA SC N   V M A D OSC

⁹Tom Thumb Crafts
1026 Davis, Evanston, IL 60201
(847) 869-9575   M-F–10-6 Sa–10-5 Su–1-5

✪ 7,000 ▱ 15 S
⬜25 ✐275+ ▤50 ⚱75 ✂75+ ▨150+ ✪1,000 ▥30
C D   V M A D

¹⁰Ink & Stamp with Sue
303 S Main, Galena, IL 61036
(815) 777-8267   Jun-Dec: Su-Th–10-5 F-Sa–11-8 (Jan-May:
Su-Th–11-4 F-Sa–11-6)

✪ 15,000 ▱ 60 C S
⬜200 ✐250 ▤200 ⚱30 ✂75+ ▨100 ✪200 ▥25
C D CA N DC   V M OSC

[11] Springbrook Farm Stamps 'N' Stuff

21352 Green River Rd, Geneseo, IL 61254
(309) 949-2787   *Th–12-6 Sa–10-5 +by appt*

✪ 3,000 ▨ 40 C
   ▢200 ✐200 ▤200 ⬚20 ✄20 ▨30 ✪50 ▥25
   CA   OSC

[12] Stampfastic, Inc

Gurnee Mills Mall, 6170 W Grand Ave, Gurnee, IL 60031
(847) 855-1050   *M-Sa–10-9 Su–11-6*

✪ 50,000+ ▨ 100+ C S
   ▢150 ✐275+ ▤100 ⬚100 ✄75+ ▨100 ✪3,000+ ▥20
   C D CA SC   V M D OSC

[13] A Stamp of My Own

360 Inverness Rd, Industry, IL 61440
(309) 254-3210   *M-Th-1-5 F,Sa-9-5 +Eves by appt only*

✪ 2,000 ▨ 15 C S
   ▢50 ✐100 ▤100 ⬚30 ✄20 ▨30 ▥3
   C D CA SC N   V M D OSC

¹⁴Marcia's Hallmark

10 W Burlington Ave, La Grange, IL 60525
(708) 352-0167   M-F–9-9 Sa–9-5:30 Su–10-5

☘ 1,000 ⬿ 20 S *Old Stamper's Samplers*
  ⬜150 ✐200 ▤50 ♨50 ✄20 ☘300 📖15
    C D   *V M A D*

¹⁵Reading, Writing & Rubber Stamps

785 Oakwood Rd, #S-104, Lake Zurich, IL 60047
(800) 842-9768   *Call–changes seasonally*

☘ 3,000 ⬿15 M C *Specialty: teachers' stamps*
  ⬜25 ✄30 📖3
    D   *V M D OSC*

 Reading, Writing &
Rubber Stamps®

Educating the World with Rubber Stamps

Free Retail Catalog

Custom Stamp Express

Custom Self-Inking or Wood Mount
Retail & Wholesale
785 Oakwood Rd., S-104 Lake Zurich, IL   60047
800-842-9768   Nationwide
847-726-8033   Chicagoland

¹⁶Stamp Thyme

201 S State St, Lockport, IL 60441
(815) 836-8180   M-F–11-6 Th–11-8 Sa–10-5

☘ **30,000 ⬿100+ C S 1-800-STAMP 93**
  ⬜**275+ ✐275+ ▤300+ ♨75 ✄30 ▦150+ ☘100 📖70+**
    C D CA SC N   **V M D OSC**

¹⁷Nickelby's
219 R Parker Coffin Rd, Long Grove, IL 60047
(847) 634-6552   *M-Sa–10-5 Su–11:30-5*

✪ 10,000 ☒ 70 C S *members.aol.com/nickelbys/stamps.html*
▢ 200 ✐ 275+ ▤ 50 ⚱ 75 ✄ 50 ✾ 150+ ✪ 300 📖 30
C D CA SC N DC   *V M D OSC*

¹⁸Mountin' Rubber Stamp Store
661 W 9th Ave, Milan, IL 61264
(309) 787-8140   *M-F–12-8 Sa–9-5 Su–12-4 Closed Tu*

✪ 2,000 ☒ 50 C S
▢ 150 ✐ 275+ ▤ 100 ⚱ 75 ✄ 50 ✾ 75 ✪ 50 📖 25
C D CA DC   *V M D OSC*

¹⁹Stamp Shack
123 S Washington St, Naperville, IL 60540
(630) 420-2254   *M,Th–10-8 Tu-F–10-5:30 Sa–10-5 Su–10-4*

✪ 15,000 ☒ 60 C S
▢ 275+ ✐ 200 ▤ 100 ⚱ 150+ ✄ 30 ✾ 100 📖 15
C D CA SC N DC   *V M A D OSC*

²⁰Jeffrey Alans
701 Towanda, Normal, IL 61761
(309) 454-7456   *M-F–9-9 Sa–9-6 Su–11-5*

✪ 1,000 ☒ 5 S
▢ 50 ✐ 100 ▤ 300+ ⚱ 20 ✄ 50 ✾ 50 ✪ 500 📖 20
C D CA N   *V M D OSC*

²¹Louella Lishnish's Luscious Little Stamps
12 N Main St, Box 789, Oswego, IL 60543
(630) 554-2378   *W-Sa–10:30-5 Tu,F–10:30-8*

✪ 5,000 ☒ 60 C S *New ideas, New stamps*
▢ 100 ✐ 200 ▤ 50 ⚱ 75 ✄ 50 ✾ 50 ✪ 100 📖 15
C D CA SC N DC   *V M D OSC*

²²Desiree's Stamps & Crafts
47 W Slade St, Palatine, IL 60067
(847) 776-9740   Tu-F–10-6 Th–10-7 Sa–10-5

✪ 15,000 ☒ 100+ C S
▢150 ✐150 ▤300+ ᪥75 ✂75+ ▨150+ ✪200 ▱50
C D CA SC N DC   V M D OSC

²³Jeffrey Alans
4601 N Sheridan Rd, Peoria, IL 61614
(309) 693-7773   M-F–9-9 Sa–9-6 Su–11-5

✪ 1,000 ☒ 5 S
▢50 ✐100 ▤300+ ᪥20 ✂50 ▨50 ✪500 ▱20
C D CA N   V M D OSC

²⁴Rubber Stamp Romance
at Gift Box, 2566 Charles St, Rockford, IL 61108
(815) 227-4269   M-F–9-6 Sa–9-5

✪ 3,000 ☒ 70 C S
▢75 ✐250 ▤30 ᪥80 ✂50 ▨100 ✪1,000 ▱25
C D CA SC N DC   V M D OSC

²⁵The Goose Barn
5311 Charles St, Rockford, IL 61108
(815) 397-9391   M-Sa–10-5

✪ 10,000 ☒ 80 C S Home of the Heat Gun Holster
▢275+ ✐275+ ▤100 ᪥75 ✂75+ ▨100 ✪100 ▱25
C D CA N DC   V M D OSC

²⁶Rubber Stamp Rendezvous
106-A W Main St, Rockton, IL 61072
(815) 624-4954   Tu-Sa–10-5:30 Su–12-4

✪ 10,000 ☒ 100 C S
▢275+ ✐275+ ▤300+ ᪥150+ ✂75+ ▨150+ ✪3,000+ ▱
70+
C D CA SC N DC   V M D OSC

27 WOW: Works of Wonder

1129 N Salem Dr, Schaumburg, IL 60194
(847) 843-0375   M-W–10-6 Th,F–10-8 Sa–10-5

✪ 7,000 ▱ 50 C S

    ☐275+ ✎275+ ▤200 ⏳150+ ✄75+ ▨150+ ✿300 📖25
    C D CA SC N DC HP   V M D OSC

28 Creative Design

119 W Market St, Somonauk, IL 60552
(815) 498-3429   M-F–8-5 Sa–9-1

✪ 2,000 ▱ 25 C

    ☐100 ✎100 ▤100 ⏳30 ✄20 ▨30 📖15
    C D SC N DC   V M

29 Paper Angel

Spring Creek Plz, 2450 W Rte 12, Spring Grove, IL 60081
(815) 675-9519   M,Sa–10-6 Tu-F–10-7 Su–11-4

✪ 7,000 ▱ 40 S

    ☐100 ✎275+ ▤300+ ⏳30 ✄20 ▨150+ ✿1,000 📖20
    D DC   V M D OSC

30 Jeffrey Alans

1602 Wabash, Springfield, IL 62704
(217) 787-7771   M-F–9-9 Sa–9-6 Su–11-5

✪ 1,000 ▱ 5 S

    ☐50 ✎100 ▤300+ ⏳20 ✄50 ▨50 ✿500 📖20
    C D CA N   V M D OSC

PASSPORT

INDIANA

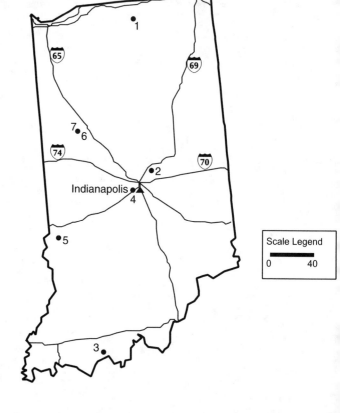

¹Ink Angel RubberStamps & Memory Albums
2104 Station Ct, Elkhart, IN 46517
(219) 295-4573   *M-F–10-6:30 Th–10-8 Sa–9-5*

✪ 5,000 ▱ 70 S *1998 Rubber Stampin' Retailer of the Year*
◻250 ✐275+ ▤300+ ☗100 ✂75+ ▨150+ ✪400 ▥70+
C D CA SC N DC   *V M OSC*

²High Hopes
44 N Van Buren, PO Box 930, Nashville, IN 47448
(812) 988-9558   *M-Sa–10-5 Su–11-5 (Jan-Feb: F-M–10-4 Su–11-4)*

✪ 2,000 ▱ 50 S *Largest in Southern Indiana*
◻275+ ✐275+ ▤300+ ☗150+ ✂75+ ▨150+ ▥20
D CA N DC   *V M A D OSC*

³The Village Scribe Shoppe
The Liberty Bldg, LL3, Hwy 162, Santa Claus, IN 47579
(812) 937-4590   *Tu-Sa–9-5 +later seasonally*

✪ 5,000 ▱ 45 C S
◻100 ✐75 ▤100 ☗50 ✂50 ▨50 ✪50 ▥30
C D CA N   *V M*

⁴Barbie's Stitch & Stamp Nook
3079 N High School Rd, Speedway, IN 46224
(317) 293-5985   *M-F–10-5 W–10-7 Sa–10-4*

✪ 2,000 ▱ 20
◻50 ✐75 ▤50 ☗50 ✂20 ▨150+ ✪100 ▥30
C D CA N   *V M OSC*

⁵Jeffrey Alans
Honey Creek Sq, 3349 S US Hwy 41, Terre Haute, IN 47802
(812) 232-3211   *M-Sa–9-9 Su–11-6*

✪ 1,000 ▱ 5 S
◻50 ✐100 ▤300+ ☗20 ✂50 ▨50 ✪500 ▥20
C D CA N   *V M D OSC*

⁶Strictly Stamps
1185 Sagamore Pkwy W, W Lafayette, IN 47906
(765) 463-1365   M-F–10-5:30 Sa–10-4

✿ 5,000 ⊠ 35 S
  ▢150 ✐275+ ▤300+ ▧50 ✄30 ✸100 ✿200 ▭20
  C D CA SC N   V M D

⁷Von's Shops
319 W State St, W Lafayette, IN 47906
(765) 743-1974   M-Th–9-9 F,Sa–9-10 Su–9-7

✿ 7,000 ⊠ 35
  ▢150 ✐100 ▤30 ▧50 ✄30 ✸20 ✿200 ▭5
  V M D OSC

PASSPORT

IOWA

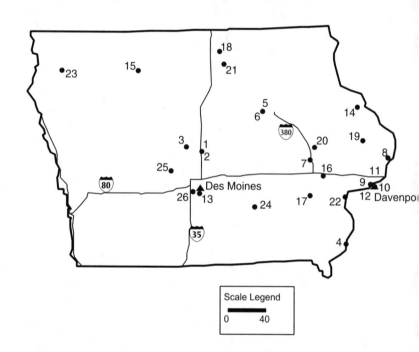

18
21
15
23
5
6
14
380
19
3
1
20
8
2
7
25
16
11
9
80
Des Moines
10
26
13
12 Davenpo
24
17
22
35
4

Scale Legend

0   40

¹Main Street Creations
328 Main St, Ames, IA 50010
(515) 233-3770   *M–12-5 Tu-F–10-5 Sa–10-4*

☉ 1,000 ⊡ 20 S
　▢150 ✏100 📋100 ⌚20 ✂50 🖼20 📖20
　C D CA N DC　　　　*V M OSC*

²The Angel's Cupboard & Toy Box
320 S 17th St, Ames, IA 50010
(515) 233-4546   *M-Th–10-7 F,Sa–10-5*

☉ 1,000 ⊡ 15 S
　▢100 ✏250 📋300+ ⌚50 ✂30 🖼20 ☉100 📖10
　C D CA SC N DC　　　　*V M D OSC*

³Bildin's Crafts
615 Story St, Boone, IA 50036
(515) 432-1304   *M-F–9-8 Sa–9-6 Su–12-4*

☉ 10,000 ⊡ 45 S *Lots of samples & ideas*
　▢200 ✏275+ 📋200 ⌚200 ✂75+ 🖼150+ ☉500 📖70+
　C D CA N DC　　　　*V M OSC*

⁴Stamp Happy Stamp Co
706 Elm St, Burlington, IA 52601
(319) 753-1387   *Tu,Th,Sa–1-4*

☉ 3,000 ⊡ 25 M C S
　▢100 ✏100 📋200 ⌚50 ✂50 🖼50 📖25
　C D CA SC DC　　　　*OSC*

⁵Creation Station
315 Main St, Cedar Falls, IA 50613
(319) 266-5321   *M–4-8 Tu-Sa–9-5*

☉ 10,000 ⊡ 100+ C S
　▢275+ ✏275+ 📋200 ⌚75 ✂75+ 🖼100 ☉200 📖70+
　C D CA SC N DC　　　　*V M A D OSC*

⁶Twin Oaks Print/Frame

College Sq SC, Cedar Falls, IA 50613
(319) 277-1463   *M-Sa–10-9 Su–12-6*

✪ 3,000 ⊠ 50 S
  ▢200 ✐250 ▤200 ⛾100 ✂50 ✠20 ✿50 📖5
  D CA DC   *V M OSC*

⁷Graffiti

2600 Edgewood Rd SW, #502, Cedar Rapids, IA 52404
(319) 396-8426   *M-Sa–10-9 Su–12-6*

✪ 2,000 ⊠ 25 S
  ▢150 ✐75 ▤30 ⛾30 ✂20 ✠20 ✿500 📖15
  D CA DC   *V M D OSC*

⁸Stamping Sensations

95 Main Ave, Clinton, IA 52732
(319) 243-4676   *M-F–10-5 Sa–10-2*

✪ 2,000 ⊠ 5 M C S
  ▢50 ✐100 ▤50 ⛾20 ✂20 ✠50 ✿50 📖15
  C D CA N DC HP   *V M D OSC*

⁹Baughman's Cottage

1105 Christie St, Davenport, IA 52803
(319) 324-8040   *M-Sa–10-5*

✪ 7,000 ⊠ 50 S
  ▢150 ✐275+ ▤200 ⛾50 ✂30 ✠150+ 📖70+
  C D CA N DC   *V M D OSC*

¹⁰Cottage Corner

902 E Rusholme St, Davenport, IA 52803
(319) 322-7984   *M–12-7 Tu-F–10-5 W–10-7 Sa–10-4*
✪ **10,000 ⊠ 50 S**
  ▢**75** ✐**150** ▤**50** ⛾**20** ✂**10** ✠**150+** 📖**10**
  C D CA SC N DC   *V M D OSC*

¹¹Graffiti
320 W Kimberly Rd, Davenport, IA 52806
(319) 386-6465   *M-Sa–10-9 Su–12-5*

✪ 2,000 ⊠ 25 S
  ⬚150 ✐75 ▤30 ▦30 ✂20 ▩20 ✺500 📖15
  D CA DC   *V M D OSC*

¹²Sue's Hallmark Shop
Village SC, 902 W Kimberly Rd, Davenport, IA 52806
(319) 391-1353   *M-F–9-8 Sa–10-6 Su–12-5*

✪ 1,000 ⊠ 10 S
  ⬚75 ✐25 ▤20 ▦20 ✂20 ▩10 ✺100 📖10
  D CA DC   *V M OSC*

¹³Stampin' Station
520 Army Post Rd, Ste 23, Des Moines, IA 50315
(515) 285-3658   *M-Sa–10-6 Th–10-7:30 Su–12:30-5*

✪ **5,000** ⊠ **30 C S**
  ⬚75 ✐50 ▤300+ ▦30 ✂75+ ▩100 ✺700 📖10
  C D CA SC N DC   *V M A D OSC*

¹⁴Sue's Hallmark Shop
670 Kennedy Mall, Dubuque, IA 52002-5258
(319) 556-1956   *M-Sa–10-9 Su–12-5*

✪ 1,000 ⊠ 15 S
  ⬚50 ✐25 ▤20 ▦10 ✂20 ▩10 ✺50 📖10
  D CA DC   *V M OSC*

¹⁵Look Who's Stamping
2205 10th St, Emmetsburg, IA 50536
(712) 852-4384   *Tu,W,Sa–9-6 Th–5-8*

✪ 1,000 ⊠ 5 S
  ⬚25 ✐150 ▤20 ▦20 ✂20 📖10
  C D CA SC N DC   *V M D*

16 Bonnie's Toys & More

Eastdale Plz, 1700 First Ave, Iowa City, IA 52240
(319) 351-1963   M-F–10-8 Sa–10-5 Su–12-5

✪ 5,000 ▱ 40 C S
   ⬛150 ✎150 ▤50 ▯30 ✂30 ▦30 ✿500 📖25
   C CA N DC   V M A D OSC

17 Mystique Creations

412 C Ave, PO Box 361, Kalona, IA 52247
(319) 656-2277   M-Sa–9-5

✪ **3,000** ▱ **25 M C S**
   ⬛**250** ✎**150** ▤**30** ▯**40** ✂**50** ▦**75** ✿**75** 📖**25**
   C D CA DC HP   **V M D OSC**

18 Rubber Stamps 'N Stuff

3573 Orchid Ave (Hwy 655), Manly, IA 50456
(515) 454-2225   Tu-Sa–10-5

✪ 10,000 ▱ 100+ C S
   ⬛100 ✎275+ ▤250 ▯100 ✂75+ ▦100 ✿50 📖25
   C D CA SC N DC HP   V M D OSC

19 Sue's Hallmark Shop

129 S Main St, Maquoketa, IA 52060
(319) 652-6344   M-Th–8:30-5:30 F–8:30-8 Sa–9-5

✪ 500 ▱ 5 S
   ⬛50 ✎50 ▤20 ▯10 ✂20 ▦10 ✿50 📖10
   D CA DC   V M OSC

20 The Stampin' & Scrappin' Pad, Inc

1101 7th Ave, Marion, IA 52302
(319) 377-1055   M-F–10-9 Sa–10-5 Su–12-5

✪ 15,000 ▱ 50 C S
   ⬛150 ✎275+ ▤300+ ▯50 ✂75+ ▦100 ✿100 📖25
   C D CA N   V M OSC

²¹Vicky's Stamp Pad
32 2nd St NE, Mason City, IA 50401
(515) 421-8387   *M-F–12-5:30 Th–12-8 Sa–10-4*

✪ 2,000 ⬠ 50 C S
　▭100 ✐200 ▤150 ▨50 ✂75+ ▦150+ ✪200 ▥50
　C D CA SC N DC   *V M OSC*

²²Sue's Hallmark Shop
Muscatine Mall, 1903 Park Ave, Muscatine, IA 52761-5400
(319) 263-9172   *M-F–10-9 Sa–10-6 Su–12-6*

✪ 1,000 ⬠ 10 S
　▭75 ✐50 ▤30 ▨30 ✂20 ▦10 ✪50 ▥10
　D CA DC   *V M OSC*

²³Turn of the Century House
102 Central Ave NW, PO Box 78, Orange City, IA 51041
(712) 737-8175   *M-F–9:30-5:30 Th–9:30-9 Sa–9:30-5*

✪ 7,000 ⬠ 40 C S
　▭275+ ✐275+ ▤300+ ▨75 ✂50 ▦150+ ✪200 ▥30
　C D CA DC   *V M OSC*

²⁴Expressions With Heart
103 High Ave E, Oskaloosa, IA 52577
(515) 672-1730   *M-F–10-5:30 Th–10-7 Sa–10-5 Su–1-4*

✪ 10,000 ⬠ 100+ C S
　▭100 ✐275+ ▤300+ ▨100 ✂75+ ▦150+ ✪700 ▥30
　C D CA SC N DC   *V M D OSC*

²⁵In My Spare Time
1107 2nd St, Perry, IA 50220
(515) 465-4468   *M-Sa–10-5*

✪ 3,000 ⬠ 50 S
　▭200 ✐275+ ▤100 ▨150+ ✂30 ▦50 ✪50 ▥10
　C D SC N DC   *V M D OSC*

²⁶Outstamping Designs
208 5th St, W Des Moines, IA 50265
(515) 277-5719 *M-Sa–10-5:30 Th–10-7 Su–1-4*

✿ 20,000 ▱ 100+ M S

▢ 275+ ✎ 275+ ▤ 300+ ⚱ 100 ✂ 75+ ✖ 150+ 📖 25
C D CA SC N DC   *V M D OSC*

PASSPORT

KANSAS

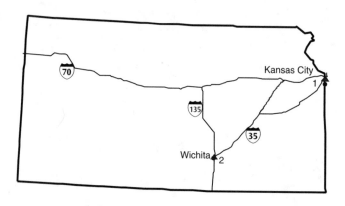

Kansas City

Wichita

Scale Legend

0   50

¹Rubber Beach Stamp Co
Mission Ctr Mall, 4899 Johnson Dr, Mission, KS 66205
(913) 236-7508   *M-Sa–10-9 Su–12-6*

✪ 7,000 ☒ 100+ M C S *We're non-cutesy!*
   ▭150 ✐275+ 📓200 ☳50 ✄75+ ▨100 ✪3,000+ 📖25
   C D CA N DC   V M

²Mrs O'Leary's Mercantile
126 N Mead, Wichita, KS 67202
(316) 262-0600   *M-Sa–10-6 (May-Sep: call for seasonal hours)*

✪ 5,000 ☒ 100+ C S *Weekly classes & Saturday demos*
   ▭150 ✐200 📓150 ☳50 ✄30 ▨50 ✪200 📖25
   C D CA SC N DC HP   V M A D OSC

KENTUCKY

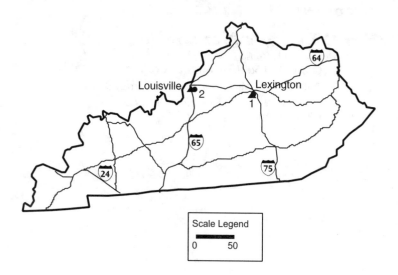

Louisville

Lexington

Scale Legend

0   50

¹Flag Fork Herb Farm Inc
900 N Broadway, Lexington, KY 40505
(606) 233-7381   *M-Sa–10-6*

✪ **1,000** ▨ **10** **S** *Visit our café, gardens, shop*
    ⬜**100** ✎**100** ▤**100** ▨**50** ✁**15** 📖**10**
      C D CA N   ***V M A D OSC***

²The Rubber Wizard, Ink
108 Fairmeade Rd, Louisville, KY 40207
(502) 894-0337   *Tu-5–10-6 Sa–10-4 Su–1-5*

✪ 3,000 ▨ 50 C
    ⬜150 ✎275+ ▤300+ ▨50 ✁30 📖30
    C D CA SC N DC   *V M A D OSC*

MAINE

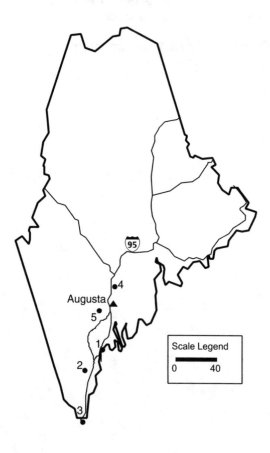

Augusta

95

Scale Legend

0   40

¹Stamps & Stuff, Inc

231 US Rte 1 S, Freeport, ME 04032
(207) 865-6685   *M-Sa–10-5 Su–12-4*

✪ 10,000 ▱ 70 C S
  ⬜275+ ✎275+ 📖300+ ⚄150+ ✂75+ ▨75 ✪100 📖30
  C D CA SC N DC HP   *V M D OSC*

²Stamper's Delights

482 River Rd, Gorham, ME 04038
(207) 893-0722   *M-F–8-6 Sa–8-5 Su–9-2*

✪ 12,000 ▱ 100+ C
  ⬜50 ✎150 📖50 ⚄50 ✂10 📖5
  C D CA   *OSC*

³Maine-ly Stamps

518 US Rte 1, Kittery, ME 03904
(207) 439-8988   *M-Sa–10-5 Su–12-5 Closed W*

✪ 2,000 ▱ 20 C S
  ⬜25 ✎150 📖150 ⚄30 ✂10 ✪200 📖10
  C D CA SC N DC   *V M A D OSC*

⁴Yardgoods Center

Downtown SC, Waterville, ME 04901
(207) 872-2118   *M-Sa–9:30-5 F–9:30-8*

✪ 10,000 ▱ 100+ C S
  ⬜200 ✎250 📖150 ⚄150+ ✂50 ▨150+ ✪50 📖20
  C D CA SC DC   *V M D OSC*

⁵Your Maine Stamper

58 Main St, Winthrop, ME 04364
(207) 377-4829   *Tu-F–10-4:30 Sa–10-2 +by appt*

✪ 5,000 ▱ 25 C S
  ⬜50 ✎275+ 📖100 ⚄100 ✂20 ✪100 📖3
  C D CA N   *OSC*

MARYLAND

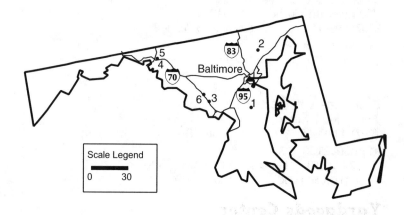

1 Inkspirations

1641 Rte 3 N, #103, Crofton, MD 21114
(410) 451-5614 ***Tu-Sa–10-6***

5,000 60 S
100 275+ 50 20 20 10 20
C D CA SC N DC ***V M OSC***

2 Trifles Rubber Stamps

2315 Bel Air Rd, Fallston, MD 21047
(410) 879-9862 *M-Sa–10-6 Th,F–10-8 Su–12-6 Closed Tu*

15,000 100+ M S
275+ 275+ 250 150+ 50 100 70+
C D CA SC N DC *V M A D OSC*

3 Purrfect Stamps

317-C E Diamond Ave, Gaithersburg, MD 20877
(301) 987-0055 ***M-Sa–10-8 Tu–12-8 Su–11-7***

20,000 100+ C S
100 150 100 50 50 50 20
C D CA SC N DC ***V M A D OSC***

Purrfect Stamps

Art Rubber Stamps Stamping Supplies

Over 131 companies!!!! Open 7 days a week!!!!
Classes, Workshops, Parties, Special Orders & More!!!!

Purrfect Stamps
317-C East Diamond Ave.
Gaithersburg, MD 20877
(301) 987-0055
(301) 987-0088FAX
Mon,Wed,Thur,Fri,Sat 10am - pm Tue 12pm - 8pm
Sun 11am - 7pm

⁴Artifacts
13024 Pennsylvania Ave, Hagerstown, MD 21740
(301) 739-3733   *Tu-Th–10-6 F–10-8 Sa–10-4*

✪ 5,000 ☒ 60 C S
 ⬜150 ✐275+ 📄300+ ⧗50 ✂20 ✠150+ 📖20
  C D CA SC N DC HP   *OSC*

⁵Howard's Art Supplies
1256 Dual Hwy (Rte 40), Hagerstown, MD 21740
(301) 733-2722   *M-Sa–9-6*

✪ 1,000 ☒ 15 C S
 ⬜75 ✐150 📄30 ⧗50 ✂20 ✠30 ✪100 📖50
  C D SC   *V M A D OSC*

⁶Rubber Chicken
19618 Clubhouse Rd, Montgomery Village, MD 20886
(301) 948-0644   *Tu,W–10-5 Th,F–10-8 Sa–10-5 Su–11-4*

✪ **3,000 ☒ 50 C**
 ⬜100 ✐200 📄50 ⧗75 ✂30 ✠20 ✪50 📖20
  C D CA SC N DC HP   *V M D OSC*

PASSPORT

MASSACHUSETTS

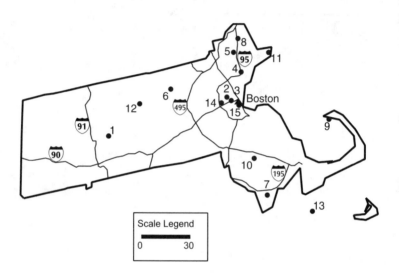

¹Simon's Stamps
13 Railroad St, Amherst, MA 01002
(800) 437-4666   *M-Sa–9-5:30*

✪ 2,000 ⬡ 10 M C
⬜ 100 📕 30 ♟100 📖 10
D CA SC N   *V M A D OSC*

²Artbeat
212-A Massachusetts Ave, Arlington, MA 02174
(781) 646-2200   *M-W–10-6 Th-Sa–10-8 Su–12-5*

✪ 1,000 ⬡ 15 S
⬜ 75 ✐ 100 📕 50 ♟20 ✄ 15 ▦ 50 ✪ 50 📖 10
C D DC   *V M*

³Paper Source
1810 Massachusets Ave, Cambridge, MA 02140
(617) 497-1077   *M-Sa–10-6 F–10-8 Su–12-5*

✪ 1,000 ⬡ 100+ M S *1000's of paper, Kool stuff*
⬜ 200 ✐ 150 📕 300+ ♟50 ✄ 40 ▦ 20 ✪ 40 📖 50
C D CA SC N   *V M A D OSC*

⁴The Stamp Lady
136 Andover St (Rte 114), Danvers, MA 01923
(978) 750-6655   *M-Sa–10-6 W,Th–10-9 Su–12-5:30*

✪ 3,000 ⬡ 70 C S *Entire line Bruynzeel pencils*
⬜ 100 ✐ 275+ 📕 300+ ♟75 ✄ 30 ▦ 30 ✪ 300 📖 70+
C D CA SC N DC   *V M OSC*

⁵Absolutely Everything
37 W Main St, Georgetown, MA 01833
(978) 352-7570   *Tu-Sa–10-6 W–10-2 +by appt*

✪ 5,000 ⬡ 70 C S *absolutelyeverything.com*
⬜ 75 ✐ 250 📕 200 ♟30 ✄ 50 ▦ 100 ✪ 300 📖 50
C D CA SC N DC   *V M OSC*

[6]Eloquent Expressions

The Village, 3 Main St, Lunenburg, MA 01462
(978) 582-6700　　*Tu-Sa–10-5*

✪ 2,000　⊡ 25　C S
　　⌂75　✎100　▮100　☕20　✂10　✠50　📖5
　　C D CA N DC　　　　　　V M A

[7]Rubber Stamping with Pride

48 State Rd (Rte 6), N Dartmouth, MA 02747
(508) 993-7977　　*M-F–9-5　Sa–10-3*

✪ 5,000　⊡ 100+　C S
　　⌂200　✎275+　▮300+　☕150+　✂30　✠20　📖20
　　C D CA SC N DC HP　　V M A D OSC

[8]Newburyport Card & Gift Shop

15 Pleasant St, Newburyport, MA 01950
(978) 462-2352　　*M-Th–9-8　F-Sa–9-9　Su–11-5　(Jun-Aug: M-Sa–9-9)*

✪ 2,000　⊡ 20
　　⌂100　✎100　▮50　☕30　✂15　✠30　✪200　📖5
　　C D CA SC DC　　　V M OSC

[9] Norma Glamp's Rubber Stamps
212 Commercial St, Provincetown, MA 02657
(508) 487-1870   *May-Sep–M-Su–10am-11pm (Mar,Apr,Oct-Dec: M-Su-10-6)*

✪ 5,000 ✉ 40 M C S
  ⌂100 ✐100 📋50 ♨30 ✄15 ▥10 ✪100 📖10
  C D CA   V M A D

[10] CT and Nee
473 South St W, #3, Raynham, MA 02767
(508) 828-1863   *Tu-Su–10-6, Th–10-8*

✪ 12,000 ✉ 100+ M C S
  ⌂50 ✐200 📋300+ ♨150+ ✄20 ▥75 ✪500 📖50
  C D CA SC N DC   V M OSC

[11] StampPort
47 Bearskin Neck, Rockport, MA 01966
(978) 546-9403   *M-Su–10-5 (Summer–10-9)*

✪ 2,000 ✉ 30 M C S
  ⌂100 ✐150 📋100 ♨75 ✄20 ▥10 ✪100 📖10
  C D DC   V M OSC

[12] Rubber Stampleton
5 South Rd, On the Common, PO Box 265, Templeton, MA 01468
(978) 939-5737   *W-F–4-8 Sa–10-6 Su–12-6*

✪ 2,000 ✉ 40 C S
  ⌂200 ✐150 📋150 ♨50 ✄7 📖3
  C D CA SC N DC HP   OSC

[13] Good Ideas
Church St, Vineyard Haven, MA 02568
(508) 693-8594   *Open year round, hours vary by season*

✪ 2,000 ✉ 50 M C S
  ⌂250 ✐250 📋150 ♨75 ✄50 ▥20 ✪50 📖25
  C D CA HP   V M OSC

¹⁴Party Needs
411 Waverly Oaks Rd, Waltham, MA 02154
(781) 893-9181   *Tu-F–9-9 M,Sa–9-6 Su–11-5*

♻ 5,000 ⬜ 50 S
    ▭150 🖊275+ 📑300+ ⚱75 ✂75+ ✠150+ ♻3,000+ 📖50
    C D CA N DC   V M OSC

¹⁵Red Dragon Arts Coop
229 School St, Waltham, MA 02118
(781) 891-1721   *M-Su–by appt*

♻ 10,000 ⬜ 80 S
    ▭150 🖊50 📑50 ⚱30 ✂30 ♻500 📖5
    C D CA DC   V M D OSC

MICHIGAN

¹The Village Stamp Shoppe

Village Inn Motel, 9008 US 31, Berrien Springs, MI 49103
(616) 471-1354   *M-Su–7-11 F–7-Sundown*

✪ 2,000 ▱ 25
    ▭75 ✐75 ▤100 ☕30 ✄15 ▨20 ▥5
    C D CA SC DC   V M A D

²Old Time Rock-N-Rubber

206 Maple St, Big Rapids, MI 49307
(616) 796-4508   *M-F–10-5:30 Sa–10-3*

✪ 12,000 ▱ 60 S
    ▭100 ✐275+ ▤50 ☕30 ✄30 ▨100 ✪300 ▥25
    C D CA N DC   V M OSC

³Apple Tree Lane

522 N McEwan St, Clare, MI 48617
(517) 386-2552   *M-Sa–10-5:30 F–10-8 Su–11-4*

✪ 20,000 ▱ 100+ C S
    ▭275+ ✐275+ ▤200 ☕75 ✄75+ ▨150+ ✪200 ▥25
    C D CA SC N DC   V M A D OSC

⁴Karen's Creative Stamping

315 N Main St, Davison, MI 48423
(810) 658-2992   *M-F–10-7 Sa–10-5*

✪ 3,000 ▱ 60 C S
    ▭75 ✐200 ▤150 ☕50 ✄20 ▨100 ✪100 ▥30
    C D CA SC N DC   V M D OSC

⁵Chestnut Creek

22079 Michigan Ave, Dearborn, MI 48124
(313) 791-0272   *M-F–1-6 Th–10-8 Sa–10-5*

✪ 7,000 ▱ 70 C
    ▭150 ✐200 ▤100 ☕50 ✄50 ▨50 ✪50 ▥10
    C D CA SC N DC   V M OSC

⁶Toomuchfun Rubberstamps
2200 Coolidge Rd, #14, E Lansing, MI 48823
(517) 351-2030   *M–F–10-9 Sa–10-6*

✪ 10,000 ☒ 40 M S
　　☐ 275+ ✏ 275+ 📰 250 ⌛ 50 ✂ 30 🎀 150+ ✪ 100 📖 50
　　C D CA SC N DC　　　　　*V M D OSC*

⁷See Spot Run
32716 Franklin Rd, Franklin, MI 48025
(248) 932-7768   *Tu–Sa–10-5:30*

✪ 12,000 ☒ 80 C S
　　☐ 200 ✏ 275+ 📰 300+ ⌛ 50 ✂ 75+ 🎀 30 ✪ 3,000+ 📖 20
　　C D N DC　　　　　*V M A D OSC*

⁸Mostly Hearts, "The Rubberstampler"
1945 Wealthy St SE, Grand Rapids, MI 49506
(616) 454-0424   *M,W,F–10-4 Sa–10-1*

✪ 5,000 ☒ 20 M C S
　　☐ 50 ✏ 250 📰 100 ⌛ 30 ✂ 30 🎀 50 ✪ 300 📖 20
　　C D CA SC　　　　　*V M OSC*

⁹Stamps N Stuff
3774 28th St SW, Grandvillle, MI 49418
(616) 532-4082   *M–F–10-6 Sa–10-3*

✪ 7,000 ☒ 100+ C S
　　☐ 200 ✏ 275+ 📰 100 ⌛ 20 ✂ 50 🎀 75 ✪ 50 📖 25
　　C D CA SC N DC　　　　　*V M OSC*

¹⁰Something Special II
97 Kercheval, Grosse Point Farms, MI 48236
(313) 886-4341   *M–Sa–10-5:30 Th–10-7*

✪ 3,000 ☒ 50 C S
　　☐ 100 ✏ 275+ 📰 300+ ⌛ 50 ✂ 20 🎀 50 ✪ 300 📖 10
　　C D CA SC DC　　　　　*V M A D OSC*

¹¹The Fabric Patch
121 N Lowell St, Ironwood, MI 49938
(906) 932-5260   M-Th–9:30-5 F–9:30-6:30 Sa–9:30-4

✪ 2,000 ▢ 20
 ◻75 ✐200 ▤20 ⏀50 ▣3
   C D CA N   V M D OSC

¹²Country Needleworks
584 Chicago Dr, Jenison, MI 49428
(616) 457-9410   M-Sa–9:30-9

✪ 20,000 ▢ 100+ C S
 ◻200 ✐275+ ▤300+ ⏀100 ✂75+ ▦150+ ✪1,000 ▣70+
   C D CA SC DC HP   V M A D OSC

¹³Stamp-A-Zoo & Stencils Too!
214 Stockbridge, Kalamazoo, MI 49001
(616) 343-0366   M-Sa–10-5

✪ 10,000 ▢ 90 C S
 ◻275+ ✐275+ ▤150 ⏀150+ ✂75+ ▦150+ ✪50 ▣20
   C D CA N DC   V M A D OSC

¹⁴Nan's Stamp Art & Gifts
49 S Monroe St, Monroe, MI 48161
(734) 384-1505   M-Sa–10-5

✪ 5,000 ▢ 20 C S
 ◻100 ✐200 ▤50 ⏀50 ✂30 ✪100 ▣20
   C D CA SC N   V M A OSC

¹⁵Stampeddler Plus, Inc
145 N Center, Northville, MI 48167
(248) 348-4446   M-F–10-6 Th–10-8:30 Sa–10-5 Su–12-4

✪ 50,000+ ▢ 80 M C S
 ◻200 ✐275+ ▤300+ ⏀75 ✂75+ ▦150+ ✪3,000+ ▣30
   C D CA SC N   V M D OSC

¹⁶The Stamping Grounds

228 W Fourth St, Royal Oak, MI 48067
(248) 543-2190   M-Sa–10-5 Th–10-8 Su–12-4

✪ 15,000 ⊠ 100+ M C S
 ◻275+ ✐275+ 🗐 200 ⧗150+ ✄75+ 🖼150+ 📖50
   C D CA SC N DC   V M D OSC

¹⁷A-1 Stamps Personalized Press

1214 S Garfield Ave, PO Box 1004, Traverse City, MI 49685
(616) 946-1530   M-Sa–10-6

✪ 3,000 ⊠ 30 M C S
 ◻75 ✐200 🗐50 ⧗30 ✄10 🖼30 ✪100 📖5
   C D CA SC N DC   V M OSC

PASSPORT

MINNESOTA

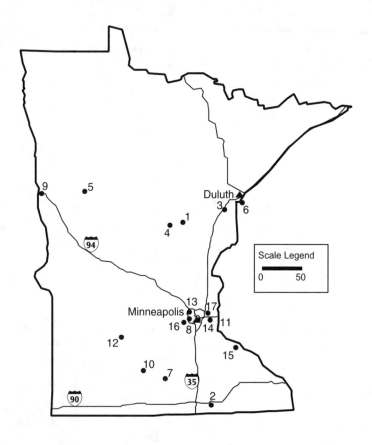

Duluth

9

5

1

4

94

3

6

13 17

Minneapolis

16 8 14 11

12

10

7

15

35

90

2

Scale Legend

0   50

¹Create-A-Card Studio

Buck's Resort, Rte 1, Box 284, Aitkin, MN 56431
(218) 678-3787   *M-Su–10-5 (Oct-Apr: open F-Su)*

✪ 5,000 ▱ 100+ S
  ▱ 100 ✐ 150 🗐 100 ⦿ 50 ✂ 50 ✴ 50 📖 5
  C D CA DC   *OSC*

²The Stamp Store

400 N Main St, Austin, MN 55912
(507) 437-9014   *M-F–9:30-5 Th–9:30-6 Sa–9:30-4*

✪ 5,000 ▱ 45 M C
  ▱ 100 ✐ 100 🗐 150 ⦿ 75 ✂ 10 📖 30
  C D CA N DC   *V M A D OSC*

³Persnickety

1854 Sheils Rd, Carlton, MN 55718
(218) 384-3367   *M-Sa–10-5 (+Jun-Aug: open Su–10-3)*

✪ 1,000 ▱ 40 S
  ▱ 25 ✐ 200 🗐 300+ ⦿ 30 ✂ 7 ✴ 50 ✪ 50 📖 10
  C D SC DC   *V M D OSC*

⁴The Stamp Cottage

24 W Main St, Crosby, MN 56441
(800) 803-1379   *M-Sa–10-5:00*

✪ 3,000 ▱ 80 M C S
  ▱ 100 ✐ 275+ 🗐 50 ⦿ 50 ✂ 50 ✴ 150+ ✪ 100 📖 20
  C D CA SC N DC   *V M A D OSC*

⁵Edwards Stamp & Stencil

HC9, Box 254, 7 m. E of DL at Cty Rte 29 & Hwy 34, Detroit Lakes,
MN 56501
(888) 588-1956   *M-F–9-5:30 Sa–9-2*

✪ 2,000 ▱ 20
  ▱ 75 ✐ 75 🗐 20 ⦿ 50 ✂ 15 ✴ 150+ 📖 10
  C D CA SC N DC   *V M OSC*

⁶The Stamping Post
5701 Grand Ave, Duluth, MN 55807
(218) 624-4722   M-F–10-5:30 Sa–10-5

✪ 7,000 ▨ 70 C S
  ⬚ 200 ✎ 150 ▥ 100 ♟ 100 ✂ 50 ▨ 50 ✿ 100 ▭ 25
  C D CA SC N DC   V M OSC

⁷Country Connection
1813 Adams St, Mankato, MN 56001
(800) 873-1781   M-F–9-9 Sa–9-6 Su–10-6

✪ **15,000** ▨ **100+** **S** *3,000 sq ft of rubber stamping*
  ⬚ **275+** ✎ **275+** ▥ **300+** ♟ **100** ✂ **175** ▨ **100** ✿ **200** ▭ **70+**
  C D CA SC DC   V M D OSC

⁸Anchor Paper Express
1104 New Brighton Blvd, Minneapolis, MN 55413
(800) 659-2127   M-F–8-5 Sa–9-2 Su–12-4

✪ 3,000 ▨ 40 S
  ⬚ 275+ ✎ 275+ ▥ 300+ ♟ 100 ✂ 30 ▨ 150+ ✿ 200 ▭ 30
  C D CA SC N   V M A D

⁹Carol's Craftique
Moorhead Ctr Mall, 5th St & Center Ave, Moorhead, MN 56560
(218) 233-3220   M-F–10-9 Sa–10-5:30 Su–12-5

✪ 5,000 ▨ 25 S
  ⬚ 200 ✎ 275+ ▥ 300+ ♟ 150+ ✂ 75+ ▨ 150+ ✿ 300 ▭ 70+
  C D SC N DC   V M A D OSC

¹⁰Donna Moe's Rubber Stamps
26 N Minnesota, PO Box 6007, New Ulm, MN 56073
(507) 359-1996   Tu-F–11:30-4 M,Th–5:30-8:30 Sa–9:30-4

✪ 3,000 ▨ 20 C S
  ⬚ 150 ✎ 150 ▥ 100 ♟ 75 ✂ 30 ▨ 20 ✿ 50 ▭ 5
  C D CA N DC   OSC

¹¹Stamp Mania
3949 Hadley Ave, Oakdale, MN 55128
(612) 770-7367   *Tu,W,F–6:30-9:00pm Sa–9-12 +call*

✪ 1,000 ⊡ 5
  ⌂50 ✐75 ▤50 ⚏30 ✂10 ▭3
  C D CA   OSC

¹²Double D Rubber Stamps, Inc
In Expressions, 132 S 9th St, Olivia, MN 56277
(320) 523-1522   *M-F–10-5 Sa–10-3*

✪ 2,000 ⊡ 1 M S
  ⌂25 ✐25 ▤10 ⚏10 ✂10 ▭5
  C D DC   V M D OSC

¹³We're Stampin' Mad
227 Central Ave, Ste 101, Osseo, MN 55369
(612) 425-5080   *M-Sa-10-5 Tu,Th–10-8*

✪ **7,000 ⊡ 90 M C S**
  ⌂200 ✐275+ ▤200 ⚏50 ✂30 ✺150+ ✪300 ▭30
  C D CA SC N DC   V M OSC

¹⁴Anchor Paper Express
12855 Hwy 55, Plymouth, MN 55441
(800) 398-2524   *M-F–8-5 Sa–9-2 Su–12-4*

✪ 3,000 ⊡ 40 S
  ⌂275+ ✐275+ ▤300+ ⚏100 ✂30 ✺150+ ✪200 ▭30
  C D CA SC N DC   V M A D

¹⁵Loons and Ladyslippers
1890 W Main St, Red Wing, MN 55066
(612) 388-3562   *M-W–8-6 Th-Sa–8-7 Su–9-6*

✪ 2,000 ⊡ 30 C S
  ⌂150 ✐250 ▤150 ⚏50 ✂50 ✺75 ✪50 ▭20
  C D CA SC   V M A D OSC

¹⁶The Quilted Bear
821 E Lake St, Wayzata, MN 55391
(612) 476-6276   M-F–10-9 Sa–10-6 Su–11-5

✪ 3,000 ▱ C S
　▱100 ✐200 ▤100 ▨50 ✄20 ▩150+ ✪300 ▱20
　D   V M A D OSC

¹⁷Country Goose
2164 3rd St, White Bear Lake, MN 55110
(612) 426-8878   M-Th–10-8 F,Sa–10-5:30 Su–12-5

✪ **10,000 ▱30 S** *Beautifully displayed*
　▱**100 ✐150 ▤100 ▨75 ✄10 ▩150+ ✪200 ▱10**
　C D CA DC   V M D OSC

PASSPORT

MISSISSIPPI

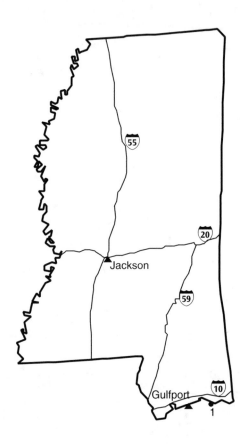

Scale Legend
0   40

55

20

59

Jackson

10

Gulfport
1

¹Stampz 'N Stuff

628 Washington Ave, Ocean Springs, MS 39564
(228) 875-4809   *M-Sa–10-5:30 Su–10-2 +by appt*

✪ 3,000 ⊠ 25 C S

☐ 275+ ✒ 50 📋 300+ ⚱ 75 ✂ 75+ ✪ 1,000 📖 25
C D CA SC N DC HP   *V M OSC*

MISSOURI

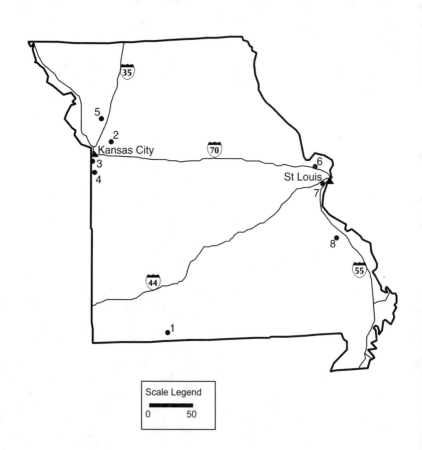

[1]Unique Impressions
Engler Block Mall, 1335 W Hwy 76, Branson, MO 65616
(417) 335-4817   M-Su–9-6

✪ 30,000 ☒ 90 C S *3-D crystal lacquer*
   ⬜200 ✐275+ ▤250 ☖100 ✄75+ ▦150+ ✪500 ▱50
   C D CA N DC   *V M A D OSC*

[2]Wacky Wagons Ladybug
451 S Thompson Ave, #777, Excelsior Springs, MO 64024
(816) 580-3434   M-Sa–11-6 Su–1-5

✪ 3,000 ☒ 60 S *Have on-line mail order*
   ⬜100 ✐25 ▤100 ☖150+ ✄75+ ▦150+ ✪50 ▱50
   C D CA N DC HP   *V M A D OSC*

[3]Paper Source
608 W 48th St, Kansas City, MO 64112
(816) 753-2777   M-Sa–10-7 Th–10-9 Su–12-5

✪ 1,000 ☒ 100+ M C S *1000's of paper, Kool stuff*
   ⬜200 ✐150 ▤300+ ☖50 ✄40 ▦20 ✪40 ▱50
   C D CA SC N   *V M A D OSC*

[4]The Stamp Patch
848 SW Blue Pkwy, Outer Rd of 50 Hwy, S of KC, Lee's Summit,
MO 64063
(816) 554-3300   Tu-F–10-6 Th–10-9 Sa–10-5 Su–1-5

✪ 10,000 ☒ 30 C
   ⬜100 ✐275+ ▤100 ☖50 ✄75+ ▦75 ✪300 ▱15
   C D CA SC DC   *V M A D OSC*

[5]Cardinal Books & Stamps
202 N Main, Plattsburg, MO 64477
(816) 539-3640   M-Sa–9:30-6 Th–9:30-8

✪ 2,000 ☒ 5 C
   ⬜75 ✐275+ ▤20 ☖30 ✄10 ▦50 ✪100 ▱5
   C D CA SC DC   *V M A OSC*

THE STAMP PATCH

Rubber Stamps, Memory Albums,
Accessories and Gifts

BONNIE FITZWATER   DONA FOWLER

Closed Monday

848 S.W. Blue Pkwy   10am-6pm Tues, Wed, Fri
Lee's Summit, MO 64063   10am-9pm Thurs
(816) 554-3300   10am-5pm Saturday
Fax (816) 554-3200   1pm-5pm Sunday

[6]Stamp and Art Specialties
107 N Main St, St Charles, MO 63301
(314) 940-9900   *Tu,Th–9-9 W,F,Sa–9-5*

✪ 5,000 ⊠ 80 S
   ☐ 275+ ✐ 275+ ▤ 100 ▨ 150+ ✂ 30 ▩ 100 ✪ 50 ▱ 50
   C D CA SC N DC   *V M D OSC*

[7]Artmart
2355 S Hanley Rd, St Louis, MO 63144
(314) 781-9999   *M-Sa–9-5 Tu,Th–9-8:30*

✪ 3,000 ⊠ 15 M S
   ☐ 275+ ✐ 275+ ▤ 300+ ▨ 100 ✂ 75+ ▩ 150+ ✪ 1,000 ▱ 70+
   V M

[8]InKleined to Stamp
at Craft Depot, 233 Merchant St, Ste Genevieve, MO 63670
(573) 883-7919   *M-Su–10-5 (Call for Jan/Feb hours)*

✪ **3,000 ⊠ 40 C**
   ☐ **150** ✐ **200** ▤ **200** ▨ **30** ✂ **20** ▩ **10** ▱ **25**
   C D N   ***V M OSC***

PASSPORT

MONTANA

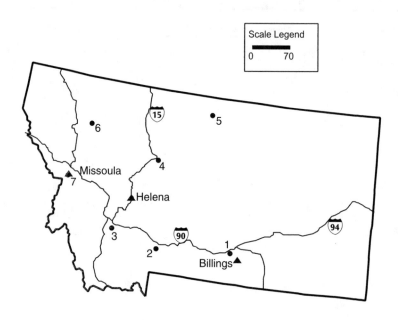

¹Stampressions
1002 10th St W, Billings, MT 59102
(406) 245-8451   *M–F–9–6 Sa–9–5*

✪ 5,000 ◲ 50 C S
　　⬜75 ✐275+ ▤200 ♟20 ✂75+ ▨50 ✪50 📖30
　　D N   *V M A OSC*

²Stamps to Dye For
407 W Main, Bozeman, MT 59715
(406) 587-1124   *M-Th–10-9 F-Sa–10-6*

✪ 3,000 ◲ 25 S
　　⬜150 ✐200 ▤300+ ♟80 ✂75+ ▨30 ✪50 📖25
　　C D CA SC N DC HP   *V M D OSC*

³Lazy Day Craft Stamps
71 E Park, Butte, MT 59701
(406) 723-2118   *M–F–10-5:30 Sa–10-5*

✪ 2,000 ◲ 10 C S
　　⬜100 ✐150 ▤100 ♟50 ✂30 ▨50 📖25
　　C D CA   *OSC*

⁴Stamp'n'Stuff/Heartlooms
105 Smelter Ave NE, Great Falls, MT 59404
(406) 761-2891   *M-Sa–10-5*

✪ 5,000 ◲ 100+ M C S
　　⬜100 ✐250 ▤150 ♟50 ✂50 ▨50 ✪500 📖50
　　C D CA SC N DC   *V M D OSC*

⁵Montana Stampin'
220 3rd Ave, Havre, MT 59501
(406) 262-9122   *M–F–10-5:30 Sa–10-5*

✪ 2,000 ◲ 15 M C S *www.mtstampin.com*
　　⬜100 ✐275+ ▤50 ♟30 ✂30 ▨20 📖15
　　C D CA SC N DC HP   *V M OSC*

⁶Stamp-A-Rama
4 River Rd, Kalispell, MT 59901
(406) 257-8267   *M-F–10-6 Sa–10-4*

✿ 2,000 ▱ 40 M C S
    ▢150 ✎275+ ▤200 ⧗50 ✄75+ ▥100 ✿300 📖30
    C D CA N DC   V M D OSC

⁷Pumpkin Carriage
Art Stamps & Stencils
401 S Orange St, Missoula, MT 59801
(406) 549-0506   *M-Sa–10-5:30*

✿ 2,000 ▱ 45 C S
    ▢275+ ✎275+ ▤100 ⧗100 ✄75+ ▥100 ✿300 📖20
    C D CA SC N DC   V M D OSC

PASSPORT

NEBRASKA

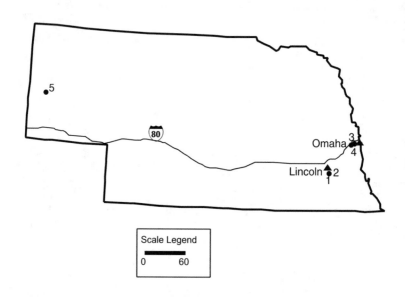

¹The Loft
5610 S 48th, Lincoln, NE 68516
(402) 421-6678   *Tu-Th–11-7 F,Sa–11-5*

✪ 2,000 ✉ 60 C
　　▭ 200 ✐ 250 ▤ 200 ⚲ 30 ✂ 15 ▩ 10
　　C CA N DC　　　　　*V M OSC*

²The Stamping Ground
Edgewood SC, 5400 S 56th St, #8, Lincoln, NE 68516
(402) 420-7867   *M-F–10-9 Sa–10-6*

✪ 2,000 ✉ 25 M C S
　　▭ 100 ✐ 275+ ▤ 300+ ⚲ 100 ✂ 75+ ▩ 100 ✪ 200 ▭ 70+
　　C D CA SC N DC　　　　*V M D OSC*

³Paper Bizarre
10347 Pacific St, Omaha, NE 68114
(402) 393-3008   *M-F–10-9 Sa–10-6 Su–12-5*

✪ 1,000 ✉ 45 C S
　　▭ 75 ✐ 150 ▤ 300+ ⚲ 10 ✂ 50 ▩ 10 ✪ 50 ▭ 10
　　C D CA N DC　　　　*V M A D OSC*

⁴Stamps, Ink
Bel Air Plz, 12100 W Center Rd, Ste 611, Omaha, NE 68144
(402) 333-2650   *M-F–10-6 Th–10-8 Sa–10-5*

✪ **10,000** ✉ **100+** **C S**
　　▭ **125** ✐ **275+** ▤ **150** ⚲ **50** ✂ **50** ▩ **100** ✪ **200** ▭ **30**
　　C D CA N DC　　　　***V M A D OSC***

⁵Little Stamp Corner
1906 Broadway, Scottsbluff, NE 69361
(308) 632-3121   *Tu-F–10-5 Sa–10-1*

✪ 5,000 ✉ 20 M C S
　　▭ 150 ✐ 275+ ▤ 20 ⚲ 150+ ✂ 50 ▩ 100 ▭ 20
　　C D CA SC N DC HP　　*V M D OSC*

NEVADA

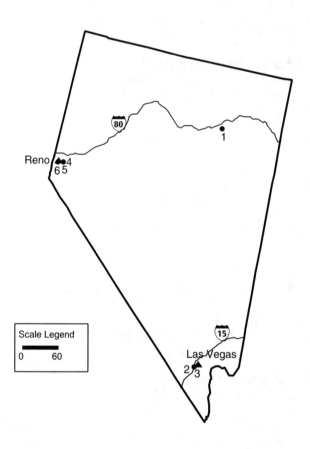

¹The Shoe Box
443 Idaho St, Elko, NV 89801
(702) 738-2397   M-F–9-5:30 Sa–9-5

❂ 5,000 ▱ 5 C S
　　▢ 100 ✎ 150 ▤ 10 ♟ 10 ✄ 75+ ▦ 50 ❂ 100 ▢ 25
　　CA SC DC　　　　　　　　　V M D OSC

²Las Vegas Art Stamps
3160 W Sahara Ave, #A-15, Las Vegas, NV 89102
(702) 367-0411   M-F–8-5 Sa–10-4

❂ 15,000 ▱ 10 M S
　　▢ 200 ✎ 150 ▤ 100 ♟ 20 ✄ 30 ❂ 50 ▢ 10
　　D CA DC　　　　　　　　*V M OSC*

LAS VEGAS ART STAMPS

3160 W SAHARA AVENUE A-15 ● LAS VEGAS NV 89102
PHONE (702) 367-0411 ● FAX (702) 367-2123

Visit our store located
less than 1/4 mile West of
PALACE STATION

CATALOG $ 3.00

E-257 $ 6.00
Floral Border

³Stamp Oasis
4750 W Sahara, V-17, Las Vegas, NV 89102
(702) 878-6474   M-F–10-6 Su–12-5

❂ 30,000 ▱ 100+ M C S *"Stamp Oasis" line of stamps*
　　▢ 275+ ✎ 275+ ▤ 300+ ♟ 100 ✄ 50 ▦ 150+ ❂ 300 ▢ 25
　　C D CA N DC　　　　　　　V M A D OSC

⁴Best Wishes

Franktown Corners, 2315 Kietzke, Reno, NV 89502
(702) 825-1500   M-F–10-6 Sa–10-5 Su–11-3

✿ 10,000 ▱ 30 S
 ▱200 ✐250 ▤300+ ▯100 ✂75+ ▨100 ✿700 📖25
 D CA SC DC   V M A D OSC

⁵Name Droppers

606 W Plumb Ln, Reno, NV 89509
(702) 826-7101   M-Th–10-6 F,Sa–10-5:30 Su–11-4

✿ 500 ▱ 10 S *Creative ideas, Great selection*
 ▱150 ✐200 ▤50 ▯20 ✂20 ▨30 ✿500 📖10
 C D CA N DC   V M A OSC

⁶Sierra Stamps, Etc

20 Hillcrest Dr, Reno, NV 89509
(702) 826-7867   M-Sa–10-5 Su–11-4

✿ 3,000 ▱ 100+ S
 ▱75 ✐50 ▤30 ▯30 ✂15 ▨30 📖10
 C D CA SC N DC HP   V M OSC

PASSPORT

NEW HAMPSHIRE

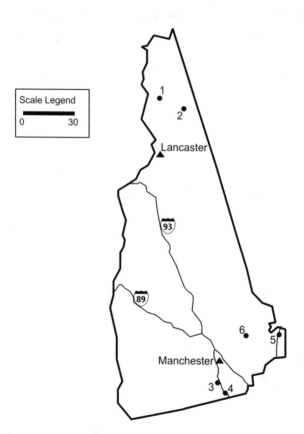

¹Fran's Craft Creations
Hughes Rd, RD #2, Box 56, Colebrook, NH 03576
(603) 237-4093   *Sa–10-1 +by chance or by appt*

✪ 3,000 ▱ 20 C S
　　▱ 200 ✏ 250 📦 150 🗐 150+ ✂ 30 🗺 50 ✪ 50 📖 50
　　C D CA N DC   *OSC*

²The Stamping Pad
16 Hurbert Ave, PO Box 270, Errol, NH 03579
(603) 482-3841   *F-M–9-4 +by appt*

✪ 2,000 ▱ 25 C S
　　▱ 100 ✏ 100 🗐 200 🗐 50 ✂ 50 🗺 20 📖 15
　　C D CA DC HP   *V M A OSC*

³Gail's Decorative Art Studio
707 Milford Rd, Rte 101-A, Pennichuck Sq, Merrimack, NH 03054
(603) 880-1616   *M-F–10-6 Th–10-8 Sa–10-5 Su–12-5*

✪ **10,000** ▱ **100+** **C S *Pergamano center, Brass stencils***
　　▱ **150** ✏ **275+** 🗐 **300+** 🗐 **50** ✂ **50** 🗺 **150+** 📖 **50**
　　C D CA SC N DC   V M D OSC

⁴STAMPede
7 Harold Dr, Nashua, NH 03060
(603) 897-0824   *Tu,W–10-7 Th–10-8 F–10-6 Sa–10-5 Su–1-5*

✪ 2,000 ▱ 70 C S
　　▱ 50 ✏ 275+ 🗐 150 🗐 30 ✂ 15 🗺 20 ✪ 200 📖 20
　　C D CA N DC   *V M A D OSC*

⁵Art Emporium
Fox Run Mall, Newington, NH 03801
(603) 431-1348   *M-Sa–10-9:30 Su–12-6*

✪ **1,000** ▱ **20** **S**
　　▱ **75** ✏ **150** 🗐 **100** 🗐 **50** ✂ **20** ✪ **100** 📖 **3**
　　C D SC   V M A D

⁶Stamp Works
23 Smoke St, Nottingham, NH 03290
(603) 679-2941   *By appt*

✪ 1,000 ✉ 5 C S
    ▢ 25 ✏ 25 ▤ 200 ⧗ 20 ✂ 30
       D CA SC DC HP   *OSC*

PASSPORT

NEW JERSEY

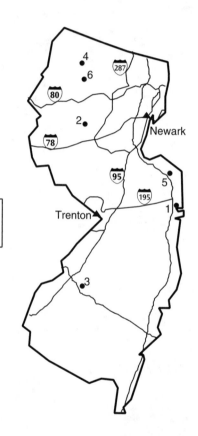

¹The Rubber Stamp Act
1005 Main St, Belmar, NJ 07719
(732) 681-7441   *M-Sa–10-5 Su–12:30-4:30*

✪ 3,000 ⊠ 40 C
　□75 ✐150 ▤100 ▮50 ✂50 ▩10 ✪50 ▭15
　D CA   *V M D OSC*

²Solomon Seals
Original Rubber Stamp Emporium, 50 Main St, Chester, NJ 07930
(908) 879-1000   *M-Su–10-5 +by appt*

✪ **20,000 ⊠ 100+ C S**
　□275+ ✐275+ ▤250 ▮150+ ✂50 ▩100 ✪200 ▭50
　C D CA N DC   *V M OSC*

³Kiva
103 Berlin Rd, Clementon, NJ 08021
(609) 627-2660   *W-F–12-5 Sa–11:30-5 +by appt*

✪ 7,000 ⊠ 60 M C
　□100 ✐200 ▤200 ▮100 ✂10 ▩20 ✪100 ▭5
　C D CA SC N DC   *V M OSC*

⁴Merry-Go-Round
19 Rte 23, Hamburg, NJ 07419
(973) 827-5578   *M-Su–10-6 (May-Dec: +Th-Sa–10-9)*

✪ **12,000 ⊠ 80 C S *Weekly sales, Free classes***
　□200 ✐200 ▤300+ ▮100 ✂75+ ▩75 ✪1,000 ▭30
　C D CA N   *V M A D OSC*

⁵The Stamp Mark It
20 White St, Red Bank, NJ 07701
(732) 758-9889   *M-Sa–10-6 Su–11-4*

✪ 5,000 ⊠ 100+ M C S
　□100 ✐250 ▤100 ▮75 ✂50 ▩10 ✪50 ▭5
　C D CA SC N   *V M*

⁶The Stamper's Emporium
at Sparta Stationery Plus, 8 Main St, Sparta, NJ 07871
(973) 729-8787   *M-F–8:30-6 Sa–9-4:30*

✪ 7,000 ⊠ 70 C S
   ☐ 75 ✐ 250 ▤ 100 ≋ 50 ✂ 30 ✸ 75 ✪ 700 📖 30
      C D CA N DC   V M A D OSC

PASSPORT

NEW MEXICO

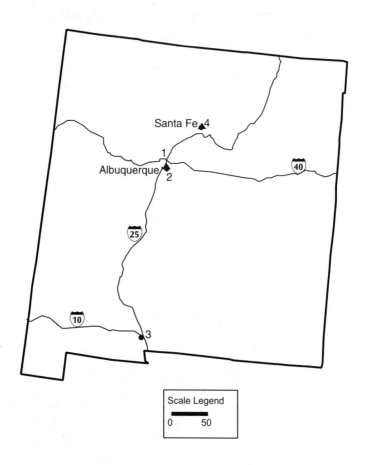

¹China Phoenix

134 Harvard SE, Albuquerque, NM 87106
(505) 255-8217   *M-Sa–11-6*

✪ 10,000 ⊠ 100+ M C S
　　□ 275+ ✎ 200 🗐 300+ ⬚ 75 ✀ 75+ ▨ 150+ 📖 15
　　C D CA SC N DC　　　　*V M A OSC*

²Papers!

Nob Hill SC, 114 Amherst Dr SE, Albuquerque, NM 87106
(505) 254-1434   *M-Sa–11-7 Su–11-5*

✪ 5,000 ⊠ 20 S
　　□ 75 ✎ 25 🗐 300+ ⬚ 20 ✀ 30 ✪ 100 📖 50
　　C D CA N DC　　　　*V M D OSC*

³Stamp A Mania

1406 E Idaho St, Las Cruces, NM 88001
(505) 521-4165   *M-F–10-5:30 Sa–10-4*

✪ **5,000 ⊠ 20 M C S**
　　□ **100** ✎ **200** 🗐 **150** ⬚ **75** ✀ **50** ▨ **50** 📖 **25**
　　C D CA N DC　　　　*V M OSC*

⁴Mail Call of Santa Fe

551 W Cordova Rd, Santa Fe, NM 87501
(505) 988-5885   *M-F–8-8 Sa–10-4*

✪ 1,000 ⊠ 25 C
　　□ 50 ✎ 25 ⬚ 10 ✀ 3 ✪ 50
　　D　　　　　　　　*V M*

NEW YORK

Scale Legend

0   50

¹Stamp Creations

1678 Oak Orchard Rd (Rte 98), Albion, NY 14411
(716) 682-3263   *W-F–10-5 Sa–10-2*

✪ 1,000 ▱ 50 C S
   ▱ 75 ✎ 275+ ▤ 50 ♟ 30 ✂ 30 ▨ 100 ▱ 25
   C D CA DC   *V M D OSC*

²First Impressions

Central Sq, 670-B S Main St, NY 13036
(315) 668-9352   *M-F–10-5 Sa–10-3*

✪ 2,000 ▱ 30 C S
   ▱ 50 ✎ 275+ ▤ 50 ♟ 30 ✂ 15 ▨ 20 ▱ 25
   C D CA N DC HP   *V M A D OSC*

³Syracuse Stamp Studio

New Country Shopping Plz, 5962 Rte 31, Cicero, NY 13039
(315) 698-2527   *M-F–10-6 Th–10-8 Sa–10-4 Su–12-4*

✪ **7,000** ▱ **100+ S**
   ▱ **250** ✎ **275+** ▤ **200** ♟ **75** ✂ **30** ▨ **150+** ✪ **50** ▱ **15**
   C D CA SC N DC   ***V M D OSC***

⁴Stampin' Frenzy

233 Mansion St, Coxsackie, NY 12051
(518) 731-2454   *M-W–9:30-6 Th–9:30-8 F,Sa–9:30-5 Su–11-4*

✪ 3,000 ▱ 50 C S
   ▱ 100 ✎ 275+ ▤ 50 ♟ 30 ✂ 30 ▨ 30 ▱ 5
   C D CA N   *V M D OSC*

⁵Fox Enterprises-The Stamping Fox

158 Lake Shore Dr E, Dunkirk, NY 14048
(716) 366-2099   *M-F–10-6 Sa–12-5*

✪ 7,000 ▱ 20 M C
   ▱ 200 ✎ 100 ▤ 150 ♟ 30 ✂ 30 ▨ 50 ✪ 50 ▱ 3
   C D CA HP   *V M A D OSC*

6Stamps To Di For
349 W Commercial St, Ste 1100, E Rochester, NY 14445
(716) 248-2420 *M-F–10-6 Tu,Th–10-8 Sa–10-4*

✪ 10,000 ◱ 100+ S
▢ 200 ✎ 275+ 🗐 300+ ▨ 50 ✂ 50 ▨ 100 ✿ 50 ▱ 15
C D CA SC N DC   *V M A D OSC*

7The Crafter's Workshop
116 S Central Ave, Rte 9A, Elmsford, NY 10523
(914) 345-2838   *M-F–10-5 Th–10-7 Sa–10-4 Su–12-4*

✪ 2,000 ◱ 30 C S *Located 20 m. North of NY City*
▢ 275+ ✎ 275+ 🗐 300+ ▨ 75 ✂ 50 ▨ 10 ✿ 300 ▱ 50
C D CA SC N DC   *V M A OSC*

8Creative Circle
10620 W Sheridan Dr, PO Box 513, Fredonia, NY 14063
(716) 672-8694   *Sa-M–12-4 Tu–10-9 W–12-9 Th,F–by appt*

✪ 10,000 ◱ 20 C S *Handicapped accessible*
▢ 275+ ✎ 275+ 🗐 300+ ▨ 150+ ✂ 75+ ▨ 100 ✿ 50 ▱ 25
C D CA N   *V M D OSC*

9The Moon Rose Art Stamps
372 New York Ave, Huntington, NY 11743
(516) 549-0199   *Tu-Sa–10-6 Th–10-8 Su–12-5*

✪ 2,000 ◱ 50 M C
▢ 75 ✎ 150 🗐 200 ▨ 30 ✂ 20 ▨ 30 ✿ 50 ▱ 10
C D CA SC N DC   *V M A OSC*

10Rubber Stampsations
3195 S Park Ave, Lackawanna, NY 14218
(716) 821-0503   *M,Tu–6-8 W–11-5 Th,F–11-8 Sa–11-4 Su–12-3*

✪ 2,000 ◱ 70 M C
▢ 150 ✎ 200 🗐 100 ▨ 100 ✂ 50 ▨ 50 ▱ 10
C D CA SC N DC HP   *V M OSC*

[11]Stampfully Yours
1927 Gannett Rd, Lyons, NY 14489
(315) 946-6042 *Tu-F–4-9 Sa–10-5 Su–12-6*

✪ 2,000 ⍓ 40 C S
□100 ✎275+ 200 ⧗100 ✂30 ▣40 📖10
C D CA SC N DC HP *OSC*

[12]Klear Copy
55-7th Ave S, New York, NY 10014
(212) 243-0357 *M-F–10-6:30 Sa–1-5*

✪ 30,000 ⍓ 10 M C
□25 ⧗10
HP *OSC*

[13]The Stamp Pad
2881 Dewey Ave, Rochester, NY 14616
(716) 663-4710 *M-F–10-6 Tu,Th–10-8 Sa–10-4*

✪ 5,000 ⍓ 100+ C S
□200 ✎200 300+ ⧗75 ✂75+ ▣150+ ❂50 📖25
C D CA SC N DC *V M A OSC*

[14]Sweethearts Stamps
8703 Turin Rd, Rome, NY 13440
(315) 337-6279 *Tu-Th–11-7 F,Sa–11-3*

✪ 7,000 ⍓ 50 C S
□150 ✎275+ 250 ⧗50 ✂50 ▣100 ❂200 📖30
C D CA SC N DC *OSC*

[15]Northern Paradise Gifts
County Rte 100, Wellesley Island, NY 13640
(315) 482-2985 *Jun,Sep,Oct: Sa,Su–12-6 (Jul,Aug: W-Su–12-6)*

✪ 1,000 ⍓ 20 S *Flora, Fauna, Faeries*
10 ⧗10 ✂10 ▣15 ❂50 📖10
D CA DC *V M D OSC*

NORTH CAROLINA

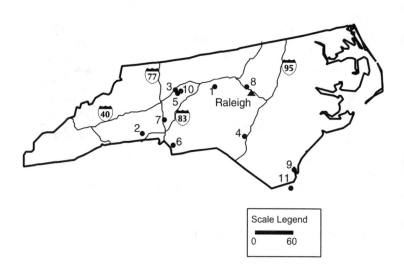

¹Chandler Office Supply

2326-B S Church St, Burlington, NC 27215
(336) 229-5861   *M–F–8:30-5 Sa–10-2*

✪ 1,000 ▱ 10 C S
▱ 25 ✐ 275+ 🗐 50 ⌇ 30 ✂ 15 🖾 20 📖 10
C D CA N DC HP   *V M D OSC*

²Cherryville Stamp Art

400-A E Main St, PO Box 577, Cherryville, NC 28021
(704) 435-8922   *Tu-Sa–1-6*

✪ 2,000 ▱ 5 C
▱ 25 ✐ 50 🗐 10 ⌇ 20 ✂ 3 📖 5
C D CA SC DC HP   *V M A D OSC*

³KT Designs Art Rubber Stamps

2665 Lewisville-Clemmons Rd, PO Box 565, Clemmons, NC 27012
(336) 766-3040   *M-Sa–10-8*

✪ 20,000 ▱ 60 C S
▱ 75 ✐ 150 🗐 150 ⌇ 75 ✂ 30 🖾 150+ ✪ 100 📖 10
C D CA SC N   *V M OSC*

⁴Crafts Frames and Things

108 Owen Dr, Fayetteville, NC 28304
(910) 485-4833   *M-F–10-7 Sa–10-6*

✪ **3,000** ▱ **15 S**
▱ **150** ✐ **250** 🗐 **100** ⌇ **150+** ✂ **20** 🖾 **50** ✪ **100** 📖 **10**
D   V M A D

⁵Enchanted Cottage

6253 Shallowford Rd, Lewisville, NC 27023
(336) 945-5889   *M–10-3 Tu-F–10-5:30 Sa–10-4*

✪ 20,000 ▱ 70 C S
▱ 150 ✐ 250 🗐 300+ ⌇ 75 ✂ 50 🖾 150+ ✪ 300 📖 30
C D CA SC N DC   *V M OSC*

⁶Carolina Art Stamps

11500-B E Independence Blvd, Matthews, NC 28105
(704) 841-2600   *Tu-Sa–10-6 +by appt*

✪ 7,000 ⊠ 35 C S *3 m. East of Charlotte*
　　☐275+ ✏275+ ▤250 ▨75 ✂75+ ▨50 ▣30
　　C D CA SC N DC HP   *V M A D OSC*

Carolina Art Stamps

11500-B East Independence Blvd. (Hwy 74)
Matthews, North Carolina 28105   704.841.2600
One mile east of Hwy 51 and ¼ mile west of I-485
(Next door to Radio Shack) Tues.-Sat 10:00-6:00
Charlotte's only full service stamp store

---

⁷The Painting Post

130 W Plaza Dr, Mooresville, NC 28115
(704) 664-5068   *Tu-F–10-5:30 Sa–10-2*

✪ 3,000 ⊠ 35 C S
　　☐100 ✏275+ ▤300+ ▨75 ✂50 ▨75 ✪200 ▣70+
　　C D CA   *V M OSC*

⁸Raindrops On Roses

8111 Creedmore Rd, #126, Raleigh, NC 27613
(919) 845-1242   *M-Sa–10-6*

✪ 5,000 ⊠ 10 M S
　　☐**150** ✏**275+** ▤**300+** ▨30 ✂75+ ▨**100** ✪**300** ▣25
　　C D CA SC N DC   ***V M OSC***

⁹Endless Impressions

The Cotton Exchange, 314 Nutt St, Wilmington, NC 28401
(910) 251-8847 *M-Sa–10-5:30*

✪ 2,000 ◲ 100+ C S
◻75 ✐75 🗊50 ☕20 ✂10 🎁50 ✪50 📖5
C D CA N HP *V M D OSC*

¹⁰Artisan's Village

3072 Trenwest Dr, Winston-Salem, NC 27103
(910) 765-4722 *M-Sa–10-6 F–9-8 Su–1-5:30*

✪ 2,000 ◲ 20 M C S
◻150 ✐200 🗊250 ☕75 ✂10 🎁150+ 📖20
C D CA N *V M A D*

¹¹The Coastal Stamper

1100 Yaupon Dr, Yaupon Beach, NC 28465
(910) 201-4153 *Th-Sa–10-6*

✪ 2,000 ◲ 25 M C
◻100 ✐100 🗊200 ☕200 ✂30 🎁150+ ✪100 📖5
C D N DC HP *V M OSC*

NORTH DAKOTA

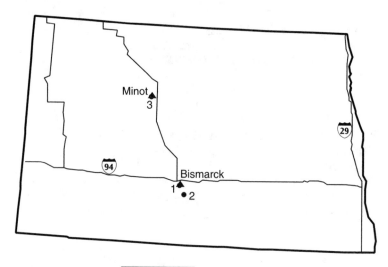

Minot
3

Bismarck
1
• 2

94

29

Scale Legend

0   50

¹Ben Franklin Crafts
1118 N 3rd St, Bismarck, ND 58501
(701) 258-7272   M-F-8-9 Sa-8-6 Su-12-5

✪ 3,000 ⌂ 20 S
⬜100 ✐200 ▤150 ⚎50 ✄75+ ▦150+ ✿500 📖70+
C D CA DC   V M D OSC

²Prairie Peddlar
622 Kirkwood Mall, Bismarck, ND 58504
(701) 223-1066   M-F-9:30-9 Sa-9:30-6 Su-12-6

✪ 10,000 ⌂ 30
⬜50 ✐100 ▤50 ⚎20 ✄15 ▦75 ✿50 📖3
D DC   V M A D OSC

³Creative Stamping
1809 S Broadway Plz, Ste W, Minot, ND 58701
(701) 852-6612   Tu-F-10-5 Th-10-7 Sa-10-1

✪ 2,000 ⌂ 40 S
⬜25 ✐275+ ▤300+ ⚎75 ✄50 ▦50 📖50
C D CA N DC   V M OSC

OHIO

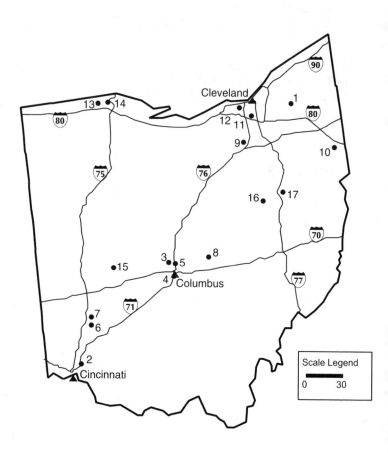

Cleveland

Columbus

Cincinnati

Scale Legend

0   30

¹Village Shop
14539 Main St, PO Box 532, Burton, OH 44021
(440) 834-9333   M-Sa–10-5 Su–12-5

✪ 10,000 ⊠ 25 M C S   *Christmas in July, Accu-cut machine*
  ☐ 275+ ✐ 275+ ⬚ 300+ ⚗ 200 ✂75+ ▨150+ ✪ 3,000+ ▱ 10
  C D CA SC N DC   V M A D OSC

²Stamp Your Art Out!
9685 Kenwood Rd, Cincinnati, OH 45242
(513) 793-4558   M-F–9:30-5:30 Th–9:30-7 Sa–10-5 Su–1-4

✪ 30,000 ⊠ 100+ C S
  ☐ 50 ✐ 100 ⬚ 100 ⚗ 30 ✂50 ▨30 ✪ 100 ▱ 50
  C D CA SC N DC   V M

³Art on the Block
New Market Mall, 7677 New Market Ctr Way, Columbus, OH 43235
(614) 792-6757   M-Sa–10-9 Su–12-6

✪ 12,000 ⊠ 40 C S *Owned & staffed by stampers*
  ☐ 275+ ✐ 275+ ⬚ 20 ⚗ 50 ✂30 ▨50 ✪ 100 ▱ 20
  C D CA SC N DC HP   V M D OSC

⁴Garnish
688 N High St, Columbus, OH 43215
(614) 224-8638   M-W–11-5 Th-Sa–11-8 Su–12-5

✪ 500 ⊠ 10 *Contemporary crafts*
  ☐ 50 ⬚ 100 ⚗ 20 ▨20 ▱ 20
  C D   V M A OSC

⁵Stamp Land
6072 Busch Blvd, Columbus, OH 43229
(614) 847-9181   M-Sa–10-9 Su–12-6

✪ 7,000 ⊠ 45 C S
  ☐ 200 ✐ 275+ ⬚ 300+ ⚗ 75 ✂75+ ▨150+ ✪ 100 ▱ 25
  C D CA DC   V M D OSC

⁶"You"nique Kreativity™, Inc
8923 Kingsridge Dr, Dayton, OH 45458
(937) 439-6692   *Tu-Sa-10-5 Th–10-8*

✪ 5,000 ⬜ 40 S
⬜ 200 ✏ 275+ 📖 50 ⧗ 30 ✂ 50 ▦ 10 ✪ 100 📖 15
C D CA N DC   *V M D OSC*

⁷Stamps & Co/Books & Co
350 E Stroop Rd, Dayton, OH 45429
(937) 297-6487   *M-Sa–9-9 Su–11-7*

✪ 2,000 ⬜ 35 S
⬜ 100 ✏ 275+ 📖 20 ⧗ 50 ✂ 50 ▦ 10 ✪ 200 📖 30
C D CA N DC HP   *V M A D OSC*

⁸The Stamp Basket
2978 Sharon Valley Rd, Granville, OH 43023
(614) 587-3539   *W,F,Sa–10-5 +by appt*

✪ 2,000 ⬜ 40 C S
⬜ 150 ✏ 250 📖 150 ⧗ 100 ✂ 75+ ▦ 50 ✪ 100 📖 30
C D CA DC   *OSC*

⁹The Rubber Room
254 S Court, Medina, OH 44256
(330) 722-2863   *M-F–10-6 Sa–10-4 Su–12-5*

✪ 7,000 ⬜ 70 M C S
⬜ 150 ✏ 100 📖 100 ⧗ 100 ✂ 20 ▦ 50 ✪ 100 📖 25
C D CA N   *V M D*

¹⁰Mellingers Inc
2310 W South Range Rd, N Lima, OH 44452
(330) 549-9861   *M-Sa–8:30-5*

✪ 3,000 ⬜ 10 C
⬜ 50 ✏ 75 📖 50 ⧗ 20 ✂ 30 ▦ 10 ✪ 50 📖 3
C D CA   *V M D OSC*

[11]Rubber Age Stamps
5875 Broadview Rd, Parma, OH 44134
(216) 398 7001   *M-Th–9:30-6 F,Sa–9:30-8 Su–12-4*

✪ 10,000 ⬠ 100+ M C S *Die-cutting center*
  ▭275+ ✐275+ ▤300+ ♨150+ ✂75+ ▦150+ ✿700 📖50
  C D   V M D OSC

[12]Creative Block
20613 Center Ridge Rd, Rocky River, OH 44116
(440) 333-7941   *M-F–10-6 Sa–10-5 Su–12-5*

✪ 15,000 ⬠ 100+ M C S *Ribbons, National teachers*
  ▭275+ ✐275+ ▤300+ ♨150+ ✂75+ ▦100 ✿200 📖70+
  C D CA SC N DC   V M D OSC

[13]Tea Time Rubber Stamps
5727 N Main St, Sylvania, OH 43560
(419) 824-5001   *Tu-Sa–10-4 W–10-7*

✪ 5,000 ⬠ 70 C S
  ▭50 ✐275+ ▤100 ♨100 ✂20 ▦20 📖15
  C D CA SC N DC   V M D OSC

¹⁴Marking Devices Unlimited
2852 Sylvania Ave, Toledo, OH 43613
(419) 475-9286   *M-F–8:30-5:30 +eves by appt Sa–8:30-4*

✪ 500 ▣ 1 M C S *Die-cut cards, Zyron distributor*

　　▭100 ✐250 ▤50 ☗30 ✂75+ ⚙150+ 📖
　　C D CA DC　　　　　　　V M D OSC

¹⁵Stamps N Stuff
827 Scioto St, Urbana, OH 43078
(937) 653-6314   *Tu-F–10-5 Sa–10-2*

✪ 2,000 ▣ 15 C S
　　▭200 ✐200 ▤100 ☗75 ✂20 ⚙150+ 📖10
　　C D CA N DC　　　　　　V M OSC

¹⁶Kids Collection
3141 State Rte 39, Walnut Creek, OH 44687
(330) 893-4122   *M-Sa–10-5*

✪ 1,000 ▣ 20 S
　　▭75 ✐200 ▤50 ☗30 ✂20 ⚙20 ✪200 📖10
　　C D CA SC N DC　　　　V M A D OSC

¹⁷The 1870 Shoppe "Stamp Pad"
199 E 3rd St, Zoar, OH 44697
(330) 874-3218   *F-Sa–1-6 Tu-Th–by appt*

✪ 2,000 ▣ 20 *100's of sample cards*
　　▭25 ✐50 ▤50 ☗10 ✂3 ⚙10 📖10
　　C D CA HP　　　　　　　OSC

PASSPORT

OKLAHOMA

¹Lady & the Stamp

127 Choctaw, Bartlesville, OK 74003
(918) 337-2727   M-F–10-6 Sa–10-4

✪ 2,000 ⊠ 15 C S
⬜25 ✐75 ▤75 ♟20 ✂5 ✪200 📖10
C D CA SC N   V M D OSC

²Et Cetera

6712 NW 38th St, Bethany, OK 73008
(405) 789-9994   M-Sa–10-6

✪ 7,000 ⊠ 50 C S *Pergamano parchment craft*
⬜100 ✐275+ ▤100 ♟50 ✂75+ ▧150+ ✪300 📖30
C D CA N DC   V M OSC

³And Bear Makes 3

4603 SE 29th, Del City, OK 73115
(405) 672-6404   M-Sa–10-6

✪ 7,000 ⊠ 70 C S
⬜100 ✐275+ ▤100 ♟75 ✂50 ▧100 ✪50 📖10
C D CA SC N DC   V M A D OSC

OREGON

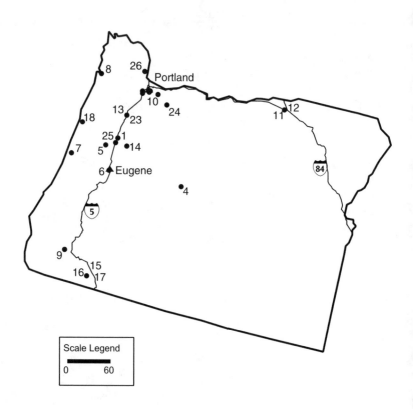

8   26   Portland
                10
           13   24
18   23
        25 1
     7   5   14
         6 ▲ Eugene
                    4

                            11 12

                            84

         5

    9
        15
   16 17

Scale Legend

0   60

WESTERN OREGON

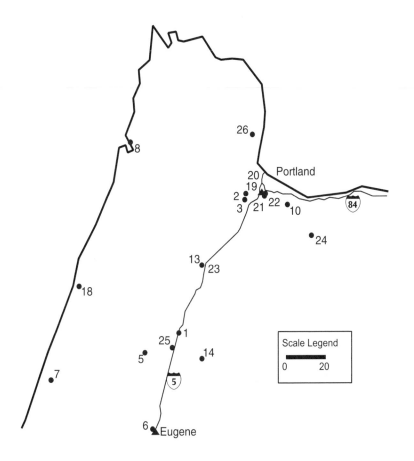

26

8

Portland

20
19
2
3 21 22
10

84

24

13
23

18

1
25

5

14

7

Scale Legend

0   20

5

6 Eugene

^{W1}S & J Stamp Designs

956-A Geary St SE, Albany, OR 97321
(541) 967-3906   M-Th–10-5 F–10-6 Sa–10-4

✪ 7,000 ▱ 100+ S *Stamping & scrapbooking*
    ▢ 275+ ✎ 275+ ▤ 300+ ⌛ 150+ ✂ 75+ ▦ 150+ ✪ 3,000+ 📖 70+
    C D CA SC N DC   V M A D OSC

²Peddler's Pack

4570 SW Watson Ave, Beaverton, OR 97005
(503) 641-9555   M-F–10-6 Sa–10-5 Su–12-5

✪ 50,000+ ▱ 100+ M C S
    ▢ 250 ✎ 275+ ▤ 300+ ⌛ 150+ ✂ 75+ ▦ 150+ ✪ 3,000+ 📖 70+
    C D CA SC N   V M A OSC

³The Paper Zone

10029 SW Nimbus, Beaverton, OR 97008
(503) 641-8112   M-F–8-6 Sa–10-5 Su–12-5

✪ 2,000 ▱ 10 S   *100's of papers for stamping*
    ▢ 50 ✎ 275+ ▤ 300+ ⌛ 20 ✂ 75+ ▦ 50 ✪ 500 📖 30
    C D CA   V M A D OSC

⁴Christmas Presence

644 NW Harriman St, Bend, OR 97701
(541) 388-4414   Tu-Sa–10-5:30 (Dec: Tu-Sa–10-8)

✪ 12,000 ▱ 100+ M C S *Many unique handmade papers*
    ▢ 100 ✎ 200 ▤ 250 ⌛ 75 ✂ 75+ ▦ 150+ ✪ 50 📖 30
    C D CA   V M OSC

⁵Paper Stampede, Inc

559 SW 4th St, Corvallis, OR 97333
(541) 753-1840   M-F–10:30-5:30 Sa–10-5

✪ 3,000 ▱ 20 S
    ▢ 100 ✎ 100 ▤ 250 ⌛ 30 ✂ 10 ▦ 20 ✪ 500 📖 10
    C D CA N DC   V M

⁶Stampit Stickit Lickit
30-M Oakway Ctr, Eugene, OR 97401
(541) 686-9997   *M-Sa–10-6*

✪ 7,000 ⊠ 100+ M C S *Huge variety*
　　⬜75 ✐275+ 📕100 ☖75 ✂30 🗾50 ✪500 📖50
　　C D N DC   ***V M OSC***

⁷Treasures by the Bay
1312 Bay St, PO Box 3123, Florence, OR 97439
(541) 997-7342   *M-Sa–10-6 Su–11-5*

✪ 7,000 ⊠ 80 S
　　⬜200 ✐150 📕100 ☖50 ✂50 🗾30 ✪300 📖50
　　C D CA N   *V M D OSC*

⁸The Ark
237-A Garibaldi Ave, Garibaldi, OR 97118
(503) 322-2645   *Tu-F–1-7 Sa–10-6 Su–11-5 (Jan-Mar: M-F–1-6)*

✪ 3,000 ⊠ 20 S
　　⬜150 ✐200 📕150 ☖100 ✂30 🗾10 ✪100 📖70+
　　C D CA N DC HP   ***V M A OSC***

⁹Stamptacular
302 NW 4th St, Grants Pass, OR 97526
(541) 471-4884   *M-Sa–10-5:30*

✪ 5,000 ⊠ 100+ S
　　⬜150 ✐275+ 📕300+ ☖150+ ✂75+ 🗾150+ ✪3,000+ 📖70+
　　C D CA SC N DC   ***V M OSC***

¹⁰A Stamp Above
68 NE Division St, Gresham, OR 97030
(503) 674-9863   *M–11-5 Tu–10-8 W-Sa–10-5*

✪ 5,000 ⊠ 80 M C S
　　⬜150 ✐275+ 📕60 ☖50 ✂50 🗾50 📖25
　　C D CA SC N DC HP   *V M A D OSC*

¹¹Lite Touch
271 E Main St, Hermiston, OR 97838
(541) 567-8294   W–1-5 Th,F–10-5 Sa–10-3
✪ 2,000 ▱ 45 S
  ☐75 ✐75 ▤100 ⚗30 ✂5 ▨10 ▦5
  C D CA   OSC

¹²The Stamp Lady dba KP Creations
158 E Main St, Hermiston, OR 97838
(541) 567-2726   M-Sa–10-5
✪ 2,000 ▱ 25 C S
  ☐25 ✐275+ ▤50 ⚗50 ✂50 ▨50 ✪100 ▦30
  C D CA N DC   V M OSC

¹³Art Impressions Plus
6079 Trail Ave NE, Keizer, OR 97303
(503) 390-2553   M-Sa–9:30-6
✪ 7,000 ▱ 100+ M C S *Factory seconds & unmounteds*
  ☐25 ✐200 ▤200 ⚗50 ✂75+ ✪300 ▦30
  C D CA N DC   V M D OSC

¹⁴Marla's Decor & More
Lebanon Plz, 2700 S Santiam Hwy, Lebanon, OR 97355
(541) 258-8707   M-Sa–10-6
✪ 3,000 ▱ 50 C S
  ☐275+ ✐250 ▤50 ⚗50 ✂50 ▨150+ ✪100 ▦50
  C D CA SC   V M OSC

¹⁵Medford Rubber Stamp
802 S Riverside, Medford, OR 97501
(541) 773-1824   M-F–9-5
✪ 2,000 ▱ 1
  ☐100 ✐50 ▤10 ⚗30 ▦6
  D CA   OSC

¹⁶Stampstruck

37 N Ivy St, Medford, OR 97501
(541) 772-5729   *M-Sa–10-6*

✪ 10,000 ⊠ 100+ C
    ▢ 200 ✐ 275+ ▤ 200 ▯ 150+ ✄ 30 ▨ 100 ▢ 50
      D CA N DC   *V M D OSC*

¹⁷The Rubber Room

2581 Jacksonville Hwy, Medford, OR 97501
(541) 770-5052   *Tu-Sa–11-4*

✪ 3,000 ⊠ 50 S
    ▢ 100 ✐ 200 ▤ 50 ▯ 100 ✄ 5 ▨ 30 ▢ 25
    C D CA SC N DC HP   *V M OSC*

¹⁸Stamp 'N Stuff

828 SW Lee St, Newport, OR 97365
(541) 265-4069   *Tu-F–12-5:30 Sa–10-4*

✪ 3,000 ⊠ 45 C S
    ▢ 100 ✐ 50 ▤ 100 ▯ 30 ✄ 30 ▨ 150+ ▢ 20
    C D CA SC N DC   *V M D OSC*

¹⁹First Impression Rubber Stamp Arts

2100 NE Broadway, Ste 3-F, Portland, OR 97232
(888) 426-8062   *Tu-Sa–10-5 M,Th–10-7*

✪ **10,000** ⊠ **100+ M S**
    ▢ **200** ✐ **275+** ▤ **300+** ▯ **75** ✄ **75+** ▨ **150+** ✪ **200** ▢ **50**
    C D CA N   ***V M OSC***

²⁰Presents of Mind

3633 SE Hawthorne Blvd, Portland, OR 97214
(503) 230-7740   *M-F–10-8 Sa–10:30-6:30 Su–11-5:30*

✪ 1,000 ⊠ 30
    ▢ 75 ✐ 25 ▤ 30 ▯ 10 ✄ 20 ▨ 10 ✪ 500 ▢ 10
    DC   *V M A D OSC*

²¹The Paper Zone
1136 SE Grand Ave, Portland, OR 97214
(503) 233-2933   *M-F–8-6 Sa–10-5 Su–12-5*

✪ 3,000 ⊡ 10 S   *100's of papers for stamping*
　　🗀 50 ✐ 275+ 🗐 300+ ♨ 20 ✂ 75+ ▩ 50 ✿ 500 📖 30
　　C D CA   *V M A D OSC*

²²The Stamp Pad
3423 SE Belmont, Portland, OR 97232
(503) 231-7362   *M-F–11-6 Sa–11-6 Su–12-5*

✪ 5,000 ⊡ 100+ S
　　🗀 200 ✐ 100 🗐 100 ♨ 50 ✂ 30 ▩ 10 📖 30
　　D DC   *V M A D OSC*

²³The Paper Zone
1880 Commercial NE, Salem, OR 97303
(503) 364-9826   *M-F–8-6 Sa–10-5 Su–12-5*

✪ 2,000 ⊡ 10 S   *100's of papers for stamping*
　　🗀 50 ✐ 275+ 🗐 300+ ♨ 20 ✂ 75+ ▩ 50 ✿ 500 📖 30
　　C D CA   *V M A D OSC*

²⁴Village Stampers
17471 Shelley Ave, Ste B, Sandy, OR 97055
(503) 668-7745   *M-Sa–10-6*

✪ 5,000 ⊡ 100+ C S
　　🗀 200 ✐ 275+ 🗐 200 ♨ 100 ✂ 75+ ▩ 100 ✿ 300 📖 50
　　C D CA SC N DC   *V M A D OSC*

²⁵The Rubber Stamp Factory Outlet
31961 Rolland Dr, PO Box 439, Tangent, OR 97389
(541) 928-3845   *M-F–10-6 Sa–10-5*

✪ **1,000** ⊡ **1 M S**
　　🗀 **100** ✐ **275+** 🗐 **150** ♨ **50** ✂ **30** ▩ **100** ✿ **50** 📖 **5**
　　C D CA N DC   ***V M OSC***

²⁶¹The Stamp Collection
34343 Bennett Rd, Warren, OR 97053
(503) 397-2259   *Tu-Sa–12-5*

✪ 2,000 ☒ 15 C S
    ⬜100 ✎200 📋50 ⏳30 ✂15 🏴30 📖3
    C D CA N   *V M OSC*

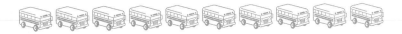

PENNSYLVANIA

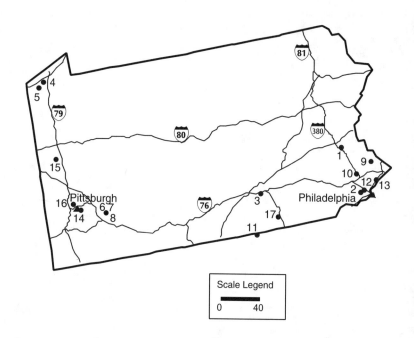

¹Knock on Wood
South Mall, 3300 Lehigh St, Allentown, PA 18103
(800) 782-6721   M-Sa–10-9 Su–12-5

✪ 7,000 ⊠ 20 C S *Complete line & mail-order PSX*
◻200 ✐275+ ▯250 ♟30 ✄20 ⊞20
C D CA DC   V M D OSC

²Create an Impression
56 E Lancaster Ave, Ardmore, PA 19003
(610) 645-6500   Tu-Sa–10-5:30 W–10-8

✪ **10,000** ⊠ **100+ S**
◻**250** ✐**275+** ▯**300+** ♟**150+** ✄**75+** ⚑**30** ✪**100** ⊞**25**
C D CA SC N DC   **V M A D OSC**

³Stamp Express
Cedar Cliff Mall, 1104 Carlisle Rd, Camp Hill, PA 17011
(717) 763-2055   Tu-F–10-8 M,Sa–10-5

✪ 7,000 ⊠ 100+ M C S
◻150 ✐275+ ▯100 ♟100 ✄50 ⚑100 ⊞30
C D CA SC N DC   V M OSC

⁴Creative Universe
6033 Sterretania Rd, I-90 Exit 5, 3/4 m N, Fairview, PA 16415
(814) 833-7896   M–10-6 W,Th–10-5 F–10-8 Sa–9-5 Su–12-5

✪ 7,000 ⊠ 60 C S
◻100 ✐275+ ▯50 ♟50 ✄30 ⚑30 ⊞30
C D CA SC N HP   V M D OSC

⁵Heritage Peddlar Shoppe
9165 Ridge Rd, Girard, PA 16417
(814) 774-4566   M-Sa–10-5 F–10-8 Su–12-5

✪ 2,000 ⊠ 40 C S
◻75 ✐150 ▯150 ♟50 ✄20 ⚑50 ✪50 ⊞25
C D CA SC N DC   V M A D OSC

⁶Art-Tech Supplies, Inc
135 S Pennsylvania Ave, Greensburg, PA 15601
(724) 832-1770   *Tu-Sa–10-6 M,Th–10-8*

✪ 3,000 ▱ 50 C S
   ▢275+ ✐275+ ▤300+ ⌘50 ✄75+ ▨20 ✪100 ▱25
   C D CA SC N DC   *V M A D OSC*

⁷Art-Tech, The Creative Art Store
Westmoreland Mall, #118, Greensburg, PA 15601
(724) 836-4238   *M-Sa–10-9:30 Su–11-5*

✪ **10,000** ▱ **70** **C S 25% off stamps on 25th of month**
   ▢**275+** ✐**275+** ▤**300+** ⌘**50** ✄**75+** ▨**50** ✪**300** ▱**50**
   C D CA SC N DC   *V M A D OSC*

⁸Kookaburra Rubber Stamps
1220 Greengate Mall, LL, Rte 30 W, Greensburg, PA 15601
(724) 838-7184   *M-Sa–10-9 Su–12-5*

✪ 20,000 ▱ 100+ M C S
   ▢200 ✐250 ▤100 ⌘100 ✄30 ▨30 ▱30
   C D CA DC   *V M D OSC*

⁹Stamp Pad, Inc
Peddler's Village, #10, Lahaska, PA 18931
(215) 794-7880   *M-Th–10-5:30 F,Sa–10-9 Su–11-5:30*

✪ 7,000 ▱ 50 M C S
   ▢250 ✐275+ ▤200 ⌘175 ✄75+ ▨30 ✪200 ▱30
   C D CA N   *V M A D OSC*

¹⁰Craftiques, Inc
Ralph's Corner SC, 2333 W Main St, Lansdale, PA 19446
(215) 855-0603   *M-F–9:30-9 Sa–9:30-5 Su–11:30-4*

✪ 5,000 ▱ 100+ C S
   ▢200 ✐275+ ▤300+ ⌘100 ✄75+ ▨150+ ✪50 ▱70+
   C D CA SC DC   *V M A D OSC*

[11]Stamp Hideaway
193 Kingsdale Rd, Littlestown, PA 17340
(717) 359-7087   *W,Th–10-4   F,Sa–10-5*

✪ **15,000** ⊠ **50 M C S** *Manufacture original stamps*
◻50 ✐50 ▤50 ♟75 ✂20 ▨50 ▥5
C D CA DC   *V M D OSC*

[12]Paper Source East
4243 Main St, Philadelphia, PA 19127
(215) 482-0900   *M-Th–11-7 F,Sa–11-9 Su–12-6*

✪ 1,000 ⊠ 100+ M C S *1000's of papers, Kool stuff*
◻200 ✐150 ▤300+ ♟50 ✂40 ▨20 ✪40 ▥50
C D CA SC N   *V M A D OSC*

[13]Stamp Heaven
Moving-Call for new address, Philadelphia, PA 19116
(215) 969-1369   *M-Su–9-7*

✪ 10,000 ⊠ 40 S
◻275+ ✐275+ ▤300+ ♟150+ ✂20 ✪50 ▥10
C D CA SC N DC HP   *V M D OSC*

[14]Stamp On It!
5827 Forbes Ave, Pittsburgh, PA 15217
(412) 422-1820   *M-Sa–10-6 Tu,Th–10-8 Su–12-5*

✪ 10,000 ⊠ 100+ M C S
◻275+ ✐275+ ▤200 ♟50 ✂50 ▨50 ✪500 ▥30
C D CA SC N DC HP   *V M*

[15]KC's Toybox & Rubberstamp Heaven
179 Main St, Volant, PA 16156
(724) 533-2663   *M-Sa–10-5 Su–12-5*

✪ 5,000 ⊠ 25 S
◻200 ✐200 ▤100 ♟100 ✂50 ▨50 ✪50 ▥20
C D CA N DC   *V M A D OSC*

[16]Stamp Fanci

460 Perry Hwy, W View, PA 15229
(412) 931-1109   *Tu-Sa–10-6 M,Th–10-8*

✪ 5,000 ◹ 90 C
⬜275+ ✐275+ 🗐300+ ⧗50 ✂20 ▨50 ✪500 📖20
C D CA N   *V M A D OSC*

[17]Stamp-ede

1720 S Queen St, York, PA 17403
(717) 852-8555   *M-Sa–10-4:30 Tu,F–10-9*

✪ **10,000** ◹ **90 C**
⬜**275+** ✐**275+** 🗐**250** ⧗**150+** ✂**50** ▨**100** ✪**50** 📖**30**
C D CA SC N DC   *V M D OSC*

RHODE ISLAND

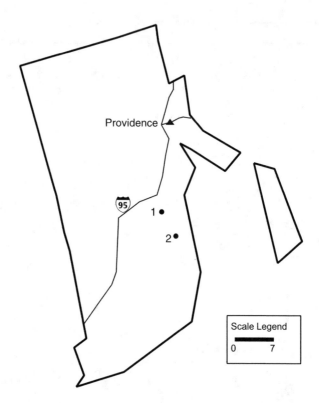

Providence

95

1 ●

2 ●

Scale Legend

0   7

¹Stamptasia

581 Main St, E Greenwich, RI 02818
(401) 885-4657   *Tu-F–10:30-5:00 Th–10:30-8 Sa 10-5*

✪ 5,000 ⬠ 50 C
   ⬜200 ✎275+ 📓300+ ⛋75 ✂30 🎌30 ✪50 📖15
   C D CA N   *V M A OSC*

²Chica Ink

29 Phillips St, Wickford, RI 02852
(401) 295-7471   *Tu-F–11-5:30 Sa–10-5 Su–12-5*

✪ 5,000 ⬠ 60 M C S
   ⬜275+ ✎275+ 📓150 ⛋75 ✂75+ 🎌50 ✪50 📖20
   C D CA SC N   *V M A OSC*

SOUTH CAROLINA

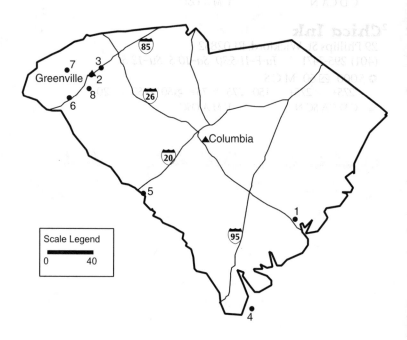

Greenville

Columbia

Scale Legend

0   40

¹Stampin' Grounds
124-H St James Ave, Near Charleston, Goose Creek, SC 29445
(843) 797-8366   *Tu-F–10:30-5 Sa–10-3*

❂ 3,000 ▱ 40 S
   ▢275+ ✏200 ▤300+ ▨50 ✂75+ ▦100 ❂3,000+ ▣25
   C D CA SC N   ***V M D OSC***

²Repeat Impressions
Little Stores of West End, 315 Augusta St, Greenville, SC 29601
(864) 467-1770   *M-Sa–10-5:30*

❂ 10,000 ▱ 35 C S
   ▢150 ✏200 ▤150 ▨50 ✂75+ ▦150+ ❂50 ▣25
   C D N DC HP   *V M D OSC*

³Melanie's Corner
2 Middleton Way, Greer, SC 29650
(864) 848-4002   *M-F–10-5:30 Sa–10-4*

❂ 5,000 ▱ 25 C S
   ▢200 ✏200 ▤250 ▨50 ✂30 ▦100 ❂300 ▣50
   C D CA N DC   ***V M OSC***

⁴Stamp Heaven Crafts
Village Exchange, 32 Palmetto Bay Rd, Hilton Head, SC 29928
(803) 686-3932   *M-Sa–10-5*

❂ 3,000 ▱ 45 C S
   ▢150 ✏150 ▤150 ▨50 ✂30 ▦75 ❂200 ▣25
   C D CA N DC   *V M OSC*

⁵Stampers Loft
501 W Martintown Rd, N Augusta, SC 29841
(803) 613-9900   *M-F–10-6 Sa–10-4*

❂ 10,000 ▱ 60 S
   ▢275+ ✏275+ ▤300+ ▨50 ✂30 ▦100 ❂50 ▣25
   C D CA SC N DC HP   *V M D OSC*

⁶The Mercantile
149 E Queen St, Pendleton, SC 29670
(864) 646-9431   *M-Sa–10-5:30*

✪ 7,000 ⊠ 40 C S

☐ 250 ✐ 275+ 🗐 200 ⏳ 50 ✄ 50 ▣ 100 ✪ 200
C D CA N DC HP   *V M D OSC*

⁷Stamp House
At Aunt Sue's Country Corner, 107 Country Creek Dr, Pickens,
SC 29671
(864) 878-5020   *Apr-Nov: Tu-F–10-5 Sa,Su–10-7*

✪ 12,000 ⊠ 100+   M C S *stamphouse.com/stamphm.html*
☐ 100 ✐ 200 🗐 250 ⏳ 30 ✄ 75+ ▣ 75 ✪ 50 📖 30
D CA DC   *V M D OSC*

⁸Calligraphy House & 20,000 Stamps, too!!
3440 Earle E Morris Hwy, Piedmont, SC 29673
(864) 295-9111   *M-Sa–10-5:30*

✪ 20,000 ⊠ 100+ C S
☐ 200 ✐ 275+ 🗐 150 ⏳ 75 ✄ 75+ ▣ 100 ✪ 500 📖 20
C D CA N   *V M OSC*

PASSPORT

SOUTH DAKOTA

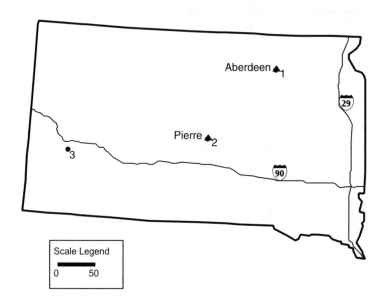

Aberdeen ♠1

Pierre ♠2

•3

Scale Legend

0   50

¹Stamp Ladies Too in Kathleen's

401 S Main, Aberdeen, SD 57401
(605) 226-0148   *M-Sa–10-5*

✪ 5,000 ✉ 20 S
◻ 25 ✎ 100 ▯ 100 ▮ 20 ✄ 20 ▨ 30 ▭ 5
C D CA SC N DC   *V M D OSC*

²Trish's Treasures

412 W Missouri, Pierre, SD 57501
(605) 224-4096   *W–1-5:30 Th–1-6 F,Sa–10-2*

✪ 1,000 ✉ 30 S
◻ 25 ✎ 25 ▯ 20 ▮ 30 ✄ 20 ▨ 50 ▭ 15
C D CA   *OSC*

³Impressions Rubber Stamp, Inc

521 Main St, Rapid City, SD 57701
(605) 343-1987   *M-F–9-5 Sa–10-4*

✪ 5,000 ✉ 30 M C
◻ 100 ✎ 150 ▯ 30 ▮ 30 ✄ 75+ ▨ 20 ✪ 100 ▭ 10
C D CA SC N DC   *V M D OSC*

TENNESSEE

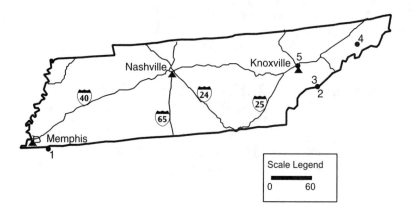

Nashville

Knoxville 5

Memphis
1

40

24

25

65

3
2

4

Scale Legend

0   60

¹Liebel to Stamp

12331 Fox Laire Dr, Collierville, TN 38017
(901) 854-4519   *M-F–9-5 Sa–10-4*

✪ 5,000 ☒ 50 C
　　☐275+ ✐275+ ▤100 ☷75 ✂5 ▨30 ▥10
　　C D CA SC N

²Rubber Stamp Gallery

Carousel Mall, Light #3, 458 Pkwy, #4, Gatlinburg, TN 37738
(423) 430-5600   *Tu-Sa–10-6 F–10-7*

✪ 7,000 ☒ 50 M S
　　☐250 ✐275+ ▤250 ☷50 ✂30 ✪200 ▥50
　　D CA N   *V M A D OSC*

³Stamps for You Crafts for Me

The Mountain Mall, Light 5, 611 Pkwy, D-8, Gatlinburg, TN 37738
(423) 430-4150   *M-Sa–10-10 Su–10-9*

✪ 3,000 ☒ 30 S
　　☐100 ✐100 ▤100 ☷50 ✂20 ▨100 ✪100 ▥10
　　C D CA DC   *V M A D OSC*

⁴Polly's Stamps and Crafts

107 Courthouse Sq, Jonesborough, TN 37659
(423) 753-9773   *Tu-Sa–10-5*

✪ 2,000 ☒ 25 C S
　　☐75 ✐75 ▤30 ☷20 ✂15 ▨100 ▥10
　　C D CA SC DC HP   *V M A D OSC*

⁵Stamps and Stripes Forever

4934 N Broadway, Knoxville, TN 37918
(423) 689-9951   *Tu-Sa–10-5:30*

✪ 7,000 ☒ 70 S
　　☐75 ✐250 ▤150 ☷50 ✂30 ▨150+ ✪50 ▥50
　　C D CA SC N DC   *V M D*

TEXAS

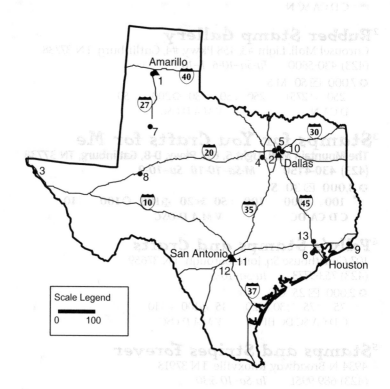

Amarillo

1

40

27

7

30

20

5 10

4 2 Dallas

3

8

10

45

35

13

San Antonio 11   6   9

12   Houston

37

Scale Legend

0   100

¹Texas 2-Stamp
3309 Bell St, off I-40, Amarillo, TX 79106
(806) 351-1111   *Tu-Sa–10-5:30 +by appt*

✪ 7,000 ⊠ 80 C S
   ▢100 ✐275+ ▤200 ⛾50 ✂75+ ▦100 ✿50 ▭30
   C D CA SC N HP   *V M OSC*

²Stamp de Ville
1014 S Broadway, Ste 100, Carrollton, TX 75006
(972) 245-5755   Tu-Sa–10-6 Th–10-8

✪ 3,000 ⊠ 60 C S
   ▢200 ✐250 ▤150 ⛾50 ✂50 ▦150+ ✿200 ▭10
   C D CA SC N DC   *V M A D OSC*

³Creative Stamp Impressions
1520 Goodyear, Ste G, El Paso, TX 79936
(915) 591-0508   Tu-F–10-5:30 Sa–10-2

✪ 3,000 ⊠ 50 C S
   ▢50 ✐100 ▤300+ ⛾30 ✂20 ▦10 ▭5
   C D CA N HP   *V M A D OSC*

⁴Eugenia's Eclectibles
5800-J Camp Bowie Blvd, Fort Worth, TX 76107
(817) 732-3608   *M-F–10-6 Sa–10-5*

✪ 10,000 ⊠100+ M C S *Dozens die-cuts & accessories*
   ▢275+ ✐275+ ▤300+ ⛾150+ ✂10 ▦20 ✿200 ▭70+
   C D CA SC N DC   *V M*

⁵Tejas Stamps
100 N 11th St, Garland, TX 75040
(972) 494-3157   *Tu-Sa–10-5 Su–12-5*

✪ 3,000 ⊠ 60 M C S
   ▢150 ✐200 ▤100 ⛾100 ✂50 ▦50 ✿50 ▭25
   C D CA SC N DC   *V M A D OSC*

⁶Stamp Times
2401 Times Blvd, #130, Houston, TX 77005
(713) 521-3899   *M-Sa–10-6 Su–12-5*

✪ 50,000+ ▨ 100+ M S
　☐ 200 ✐ 275+ ▤ 200 ☱ 50 ✂ 75+ ▧ 50 ✪ 300 ▥ 25
　C D CA SC N   *V M A D*

⁷That Stamp Store
4511 34th St, #5004, Lubbock, TX 79414
(806) 792-8834   *M-Sa–11-6 Su–1-5*

✪ 5,000 ▨ 30 S
　☐ 50 ✐ 150 ▤ 250 ☱ 75 ✂ 75+ ▧ 50 ✪ 200 ▥ 70+
　C D CA SC N DC   *V M A D OSC*

⁸The Crazy Stamper
3411 Trinity Meadows, Midland, TX 79707
(915) 520-8329   *By appt only*

✪ 2,000 ▨ 25 S
　☐ 75 ✐ 150 ▤ 50 ☱ 10 ✂ 50 ▧ 20 ▥ 20
　C D CA SC N DC   *V M D*

⁹B & G Rubber Stamp Store
139 Nederland Ave, Nederland, TX 77627
(409) 727-5728   *Call for hours*

✪ 3,000 ▨ 50
　☐ 150 ✐ 275+ ▤ 100 ☱ 75 ✂ 50 ▧ 30 ✪ 50 ▥ 10
　C D CA SC N DC   *V M A D OSC*

¹⁰Stamp Asylum
2001 Coit Rd, Ste 165, Plano, TX 75075
(972) 596-1224   *M-F–10-6 Sa–10-5*

✪ 30,000+ ▨ 100+ M C S
　☐ 275+ ✐ 275+ ▤ 300+ ☱ 150+ ✂ 50 ▧ 20 ✪ 200 ▥ 70+
　C D CA SC N DC   *V M D OSC*

¹¹Lone Star Stamps
10918 Wurzbach, Ste 127, San Antonio, TX 78230
(210) 690-2058   *Tu-F–10-6 Sa–10-5*

✪ 10,000 ⌧ 100+ C S
   ⬚150 ✐275+ ▤150 ⚱50 ✂30 ▨100 ✿200 ▱30
   C D CA SC N DC   *V M D*

¹²Stamp Antonio
1931 NW Military Hwy, San Antonio, TX 78213
(210) 342-6217   *M-Sa–10-6 Th-10-7*

✪ **50,000+** ⌧ **100+ M C S**
   ⬚**150** ✐**275+** ▤**150** ⚱**100** ✂**30** ▨**75** ✿**50** ▱**20**
   C D CA N DC   *V M D*

¹³Eccentricities
315 Gentry St, #C-7, Spring, TX 77373
(281) 288-0585   *M-Sa–10-5 Su–12-5*

✪ 3,000 ⌧ 80 S *Pergamano, Papermaking*
   ⬚150 ✐100 ▤200 ⚱100 ✂75+ ▨75 ✿500 ▱30
   C D CA SC N DC   *V M A D OSC*

PASSPORT

UTAH

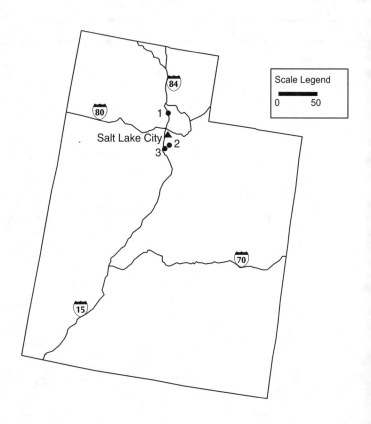

¹Stamping Station
253 S Main, Layton, UT 84041
(801) 543-0123   M-F–10-7 Sa–10-6

✪ 5,000 ▱ 40 M C S
 ▭100 ✐150 ▤300+ ⧗20 ✄50 ✠100 ❁300 📖15
 C D CA SC N DC   V M

²Stamps, Etc
at Paper Hearts, 6185 Highland, Salt Lake City, UT 84121
(801) 272-2280   M–10-6 Tu-Sa–10-8

✪ 5,000 ▱ 80 S
 ▭275+ ✐250 ▤300+ ⧗75 ✄75+ ✠150+ ❁1,000 📖70+
 C D CA N DC   V M D OSC

³Jayhawk Rubber Stamp Co
10578 S 700 E, Sandy, UT 84070
(801) 495-3677   M-F–12-6 Sa–12-5 Closed W

✪ 2,000 ▱1 M
 ▭25 ▤30 ⧗10 ✠10 📖3
 D CA N HP   V M A D OSC

VERMONT

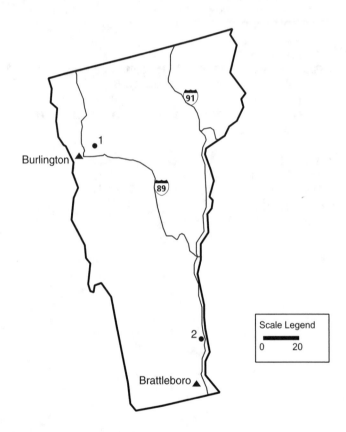

¹Stamp On It

Towne Marketplace, #20, (off Suzy Wilson Rd), Essex Junction, VT 05452

(802) 872-0877   *M-Sa–10-5:30 F–10-7 Su–12-4*

✪ 3,000 ⌂ 40 C S

◻150 ✎275+ ▤50 ▯50 ✂50 ▨150+ ✪100 ▥30

C D CA SC N DC   *V M OSC*

²Rubber Stamps of America

Warner Ctr, Westminster St, PO Box 567, Saxtons River, VT 05154

(802) 869-2622   *M-F–9-5 Sa–10-4*

✪ 2,000 ⌂ 5 M C *RSA & Ken Brown Stamps*

◻50 ✎25 ▤10 ▯20 ✂7 ▨10 ▥3

C CA N HP   *V M A D OSC*

VIRGINIA

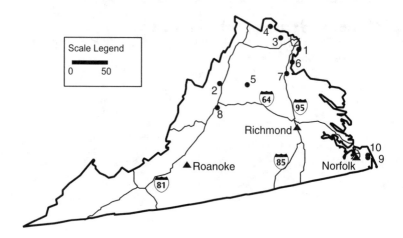

¹A Likely Story

1555 King St, Alexandria, VA 22314
(703) 836-2498   *M-Sa–10-6 Su–1-5*

✪ 500 ⊠ 20 C
    ⬜ 25 🗐 10 🥄 10 ✂ 3 ✪ 100 📖 3
    C D CA SC   *V M OSC*

²The Craft House/Studio Artshop

at Studio Art Shop, 313- C Neff Ave, Harrisonburg, VA 22801
(540) 432-0695   *M-F–9-8 Sa–9-5*

✪ 5,000 ⊠ 10 S
    ⬜ 275+ ✏ 275+ 🗐 300+ 🥄 100 ✂ 100 🔲 150+ ✪ 300 📖 50
    C D   *V M A D OSC*

³Artfully Scribed

719 Pine St, PO Box 5093, Herndon, VA 20170
(703) 787-8267   *Tu-Th–11-6 F–11-8 Sa–11-5*

✪ **7,000** ⊠ **90** **C S *Stamp exchange, Calligraphy classes***
    ⬜ **200** ✏ **275+** 🗐 **200** 🥄 **75** ✂ **75+** 🔲 **50** ✪ **200** 📖 **50**

    C D CA SC N DC   *V M D OSC*

⁴The Stamp Gallery
Southern Exchange, 312-E Market St (Rte 7), Leesburg, VA 20176
(703) 779-2447   M-Sa–10-6 Su–12-5

✪ 1,000 ⊠ 20 C S
　□75 ✐150 ▤50 ⌖75 ✄10 ▧10 ▭15
　C D CA   V M D OSC

⁵Handcraft House
US Rte 29, 2 miles S of Madison, RR1, Box 104-BD, Madison, VA 22727
(540) 948-6323   M-Sa–10-5:30 Su–1-5:30

✪ 2,000 ⊠ 25 S
　□150 ✐150 ▤150 ⌖30 ✄20 ▧30 ▭20
　C D CA N DC   V M D OSC

⁶Milltown Obsessions
305 Mill St, Occoquan, VA 22125
(703) 490-6680   M-Su–10-5

✪ **15,000** ⊠ **100+** **M C S** *"Widest range of stamps"*
　□**275+** ✐**200** ▤**200** ⌖**150+** ✄**50** ▧**20** ▭**20**
　C D CA N DC   **V M D OSC**

⁷Friends of the Library Gift Shop
2001 Parkway Blvd, Stafford, VA 22554
(540) 659-4909   May-Sep: M-Th–9-9 F,Sa–9-5:30 +(Oct-Apr: Su 1-5)

✪ 2,000 ⊠ 15 C S
　□50 ✐275+ ▤20 ⌖20 ▧20 ✪200 ▭10
　C SC DC   V M A D OSC

⁸Sonshine Rubber Stamps
Route 250 W, Exit 222 off I-81, PO Box 2425, Staunton, VA 24402
(540) 248-1111   M-F–10-6 Sa–10-4

✪ 3,000 ⊠ 25 C
　□100 ✐150 ▤20 ⌖100 ✄50 ▧50
　C D CA DC   OSC

⁹Stamp It!
317 Laskin Rd, Virginia Beach, VA 23451
(757) 425-0721   M-F–10-6 Sa–9-5

✪ 10,000 ◪ 80 M C S *Largest stamp store in VA*
　▢ 150 ✎ 275+ ▤ 100 ♨ 30 ✂ 30 ▩ 75 ▥ 30
　　C D DC   V M D OSC

¹⁰Stamper's Paradise
2135 General Booth Blvd, #136, Virginia Beach, VA 23454
(757) 563-9898   M-Sa–10-8 Su–12-6

✪ 10,000 ◪ 100+ S
　▢ 250 ✎ 250 ▤ 250 ♨ 100 ✂ 50 ▩ 150+ ✪ 1,000 ▥ 30
　　C D CA SC N DC   V M OSC

PASSPORT

WASHINGTON

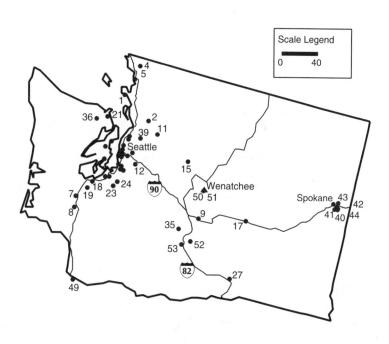

Scale Legend

0   40

4
5
1
36   21
2
39   11
Seattle
12
15
50 51   Wenatchee
7   18
19   23   24
90
8
9
35
17
53   52
82
27
49

Spokane 43
41 40   42
44

SEATTLE AREA

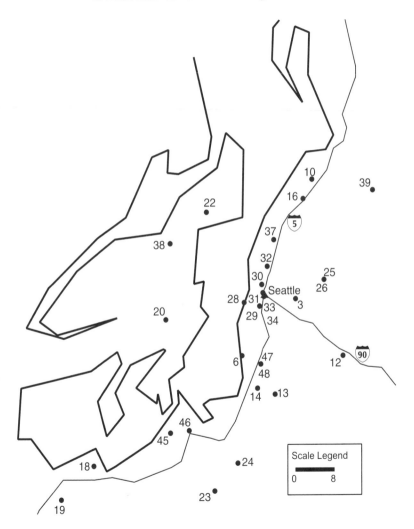

[1]Dewey, Inkum & Howe
414 Commercial Ave, Anacortes, WA 98221
(360) 293-2500   *Tu-Sa–10-5*

♻ 3,000 ▱ 70 M S
　　▭ 250 ✏ 275+ 📕 50 ⚱ 30 ✂ 20 ✠ 10 ♻ 50 📖 20
　　C D CA SC N DC HP   *V M D OSC*

[2]Crystal Creations
23727 19th Ave NE, Arlington, WA 98223
(360) 435-8327   *Tu-Sa–10-6 +eve classes*

♻ 5,000 ▱ 45 M C S *Wholesale/Retail scented E P*
　　▭ 50 ✏ 275+ 📕 300+ ⚱ 100 ✂ 30 ✠ 75 ♻ 50 📖 70+
　　C D CA SC N   V M A D OSC

[3]Impress Rubber Stamps
258-A Bellevue Sq, Bellevue, WA 98004
(425) 453-2748   *M-Sa–9:30-9:30 Su–11-6*

♻ 20,000 ▱ 100+ M C S
　　▭ 75 ✏ 200 📕 100 ⚱ 50 ✂ 50 ✠ 75 📖 50
　　C D N   *V M*

[4]Stampadoodle
915 Iowa St, Bellingham, WA 98225
(360) 647-9663   *M-Th–9-6 F,Sa–9-7 Su–11-5*

♻ 50,000+ ▱ 100+ C S
　　▭ 250 ✏ 275+ 📕 300+ ⚱ 75 ✂ 75+ ✠ 150+ ♻ 3,000+ 📖 70+
　　C D CA N DC   *V M A D OSC*

[5]The Paper Zone
915 Iowa St, Bellingham, WA 98225
(360) 671-3755   *M-F–8-6 Sa–10-5 Su–11-4*

♻ 2,000 ▱ 10 S *100's of papers for stamping*
　　▭   ✏ 275+ 📕 300+ ⚱   ✂ 75+ ✠ 50 ♻ 500 📖 30
　　C D CA   *V M A D OSC*

⁶Inkpotpourri
152 SW 153rd St, Burien, WA 98166
(206) 248-5132   *M-Sa–10-6*

✪ 5,000 ⊠ 80 C S
  ☐200 ✐275+ 📋100 🏺50 ✂10 🧵150+ ✪50 📖20
  C D CA SC N DC   *V M OSC*

⁷Love 2 Stamp
1125 Harrison Ave by Outlet Centers, Just off freeway (Harrison
exit), Centralia, WA 98537
(360) 736-9535   *M-Sa–10:30-6*

✪ 7,000 ⊠ 30 M S
  ☐150 ✐200 📋300+ 🏺50 ✂30 🧵10 ✪300 📖30
  C D CA SC N DC HP   *V M A D OSC*

Love to Stamp

Thousands of stamps and
Scrap booking supplies
1125 Harrison Ave.
Centralia WA. 98531
(360) 736-9535
http://www.cen.quik.com/stamps/
Next to Safeway, by outlets

Olympia
Harrison Exit
left at 1st light
I⁵
x
Portland

⁸Book 'N Brush
518 N Market Blvd, Chehalis, WA 98532
(360) 748-6221   *M-Th–9-5:30 F–9-6 Sa–10-5:30*

✪ 3,000 ⊠ 30 S
  ☐150 ✐275+ 📋100 🏺100 ✂75+ 🧵150+ 📖10
  C D N DC   *V M D OSC*

⁹Rubber Stamp Expressions
315½ N Main, Ellensburg, WA 98926
(509) 925-7505   *M-F–10-5:30   Sa–10-4*

✪ 2,000 ⊠ 90 M C S
    ☐ 50 ✐ 75 ▊ 150 ⸙ 100 ✂ 75+ ✠ 100 ✪ 200 ▭ 20
    C D CA DC   *V M A D OSC*

¹⁰The Paper Zone
9423 Evergreen Way, Everett, WA 98204
(425) 355-7703   *M-F–8-7   Sa,Su–10-6*

✪ 2,000 ⊠ 10 S *100's of papers for stamping*
    ☐ 50 ✐ 275+ ▊ 300+ ⸙ 20 ✂ 75+ ✠ 50 ✪ 500 ▭ 30
    C D CA   *V M A D OSC*

¹¹My Country Dream
109 N Granite Ave, PO Box 540, Granite Falls, WA 98252
(360) 691-6511   *Tu-F–11-6   Sa–11-5   (+ Su Tu-F–10-8 Jun-Aug,Dec–call)*

✪ 1,000 ⊠ 15 C S
    ☐ 100 ✐ 200 ▊ 150 ⸙ 20 ✂ 30 ✠ 20 ✪ 50 ▭ 25
    C D CA N   *V M OSC*

¹²Make An Impression
Gilman Village, 317 NW Gilman Blvd, Ste 16, Issaquah, WA 98027
(425) 557-9247   *M-Sa–10-6   Th,F–10-8   Su–11-5   Closed Tu*

✪ 20,000 ⊠ 100+ M C S **Largest in the Northwest**
    ☐ 275+ ✐ 275+ ▊ 200 ⸙ 75 ✂ 75+ ✠ 150+ ✪ 500 ▭ 50
    C D CA N DC   *V M A D OSC*

¹³alota Rubber Stamps
12920 Kent Kangley Rd, Kent, WA 98031
(253) 630-7810   *M-F–10-6   Th–10-9   Sa–10-4   Su–11-4*

✪ 5,000 ⊠ 100+ M C S
    ☐ 150 ✐ 150 ▊ 200 ⸙ 75 ✂ 50 ✠ 10 ▭ 10
    C D CA SC N DC   *V M OSC*

[14]Sweet Impressions, Inc

218 1st Ave S, Kent, WA 98032
(253) 852-6722   *Tu-Sa–10-6*

✿ 3,000 ☒ 30 M S
  ▢ 100 ✎ 150 ▥ 100 ☷ 30 ✂ 30 ▨ 100 ✿ 100 ▭ 50
  C D CA N DC   *V M OSC*

[15]Images, Sounds & Rubber Stamps II

821 B Front St, PO Box 624, Leavenworth, WA 98826
(509) 548-5656   *M-Su–10-5*

✿ 2,000 ☒ 15 M C S
  ▢ 200 ✎ 275+ ▥ 100 ☷ 50 ✂ 30 ▨ 50 ▭ 20
  C D CA   *V M A D OSC*

[16]Fun Stamps (formerly Stampeeze)

18411 Alderwood Mall Pkwy, Ste F, Lynnwood, WA 98037
(425) 670-6759   *M-Sa–10-8 Su–12-5*

✿ 30,000 ☒ 100+ M C S
  ▢ 50 ✎ 275+ ▥ 100 ☷ 50 ✂ 50 ▨ 50 ✿ 200 ▭ 50
  C D CA SC N DC   *V M D OSC*

[17]The Rubber Stamp Connection
106 W 3rd Ave, Moses Lake, WA 98837
(509) 765-8089   *M-F–10-5:30 Sa–10-5*

✪ 2,000 ▱ 40 C S
   ▭150 ✐200 ▤300+ ♟50 ✄30 ▨20 ✿50 📖10
   C D CA N   *V M OSC*

[18]Inky Fingers
7905 Martin Way, Olympia, WA 98516
(360) 438-1935   *M-F–10-5:30 Sa–10-4*

✪ 10,000 ▱ 30 S
   ▭50 ✐275+ ▤100 ♟50 ✄75+ ▨50 📖50
   C D CA SC N DC   *V M A D OSC*

[19]Quackers
215 5th Ave SE, Olympia, WA 98501
(360) 357-6820   *M-F–10-6 Su–12-5*

✪ 5,000 ▱ 80 C S
   ▭200 ✐275+ ▤150 ♟100 ✄50 ▨75 ✿100 📖25
   C D CA N   *V M D OSC*

[20]Wandakins
1703 SE Sedgewick Rd, #115, Port Orchard, WA 98366
(360) 876-4465   *M-F–9:30-6 Sa–10-5*

✪ **20,000 ▱ 90 M C S *Friendly hands-on store***
   ▭150 ✐275+ ▤300+ ♟50 ✄50 ▨150+ ✿3,000+ 📖25
   C D CA SC N DC   *V M OSC*

[21]The Stamp Cottage
940 Water St, Port Townsend, WA 98368
(360) 379-6801   *M-Su–10:30-5:30 (Jul-Sept: M-Su–10:30-8)*

✪ 3,000 ▱ 30 C S *Scrapbooking room, Beanie Babies*
   ▭250 ✐275+ ▤300+ ♟40 ✄75+ ✿300 📖10
   C D N DC   *V M D OSC*

²²Rubber Soul
18830-A Front St, PO Box 2849, Poulsbo, WA 98370
(360) 779-7757   *M-Sa–10-6 Su–11-5*

✿ 7,000 ▱ 100+ M C S
　▱ 100 ✐ 275+ ▤ 200 ♜ 100 ✂ 50 ▨ 100 ▥ 50
　C D CA SC N DC   *V M A D OSC*

²³Puyallup Creative Stamping
11014 94th Ave E, Ste D, Puyallup, WA 98373
(253) 848-7289   *M-F–10-6 Sa–10-5*

✿ 12,000 ▱ 20 S
　▱ 50 ✐ 275+ ▤ 250 ♜ 50 ✂ 75+ ▨ 100 ✿ 100 ▥ 15
　C D CA SC N DC   *V M A D OSC*

²⁴Stamptastic
2817 E Main Ave, Puyallup, WA 98372
(253) 770-6240   *M-Sa–10-6*

✿ 3,000 ▱ 60 M C S
　▱ 150 ✐ 250 ▤ 150 ♜ 30 ✂ 10 ▨ 10 ✿ 50 ▥ 15
　C D CA SC DC   *V M OSC*

²⁵Rubber Soul
Redmond Town Ctr, 16444 NE 74th St, Redmond, WA 98052
(425) 882-3333   *M-Sa–10-8 Su–11-6*

✿ 7,000 ▱ 100+ M C S
　▱ 100 ✐ 275+ ▤ 200 ♜ 100 ✂ 50 ▨ 100 ▥ 50
　C D CA SC N DC   *V M A D OSC*

²⁶The Paper Zone
3828 148th Ave NE, Redmond, WA 98052
(425) 883-0273   *M-F–8-6 Sa–10-5 Su–12-5*

✿ 2,000 ▱ 10 S *100's of papers for stamping*
　▱ 50 ✐ 275+ ▤ 300+ ♜ 20 ✂ 75+ ▨ 50 ✿ 500 ▥ 30
　C D CA   *V M A D OSC*

²⁷PSS Rubber Stamps
1341-D George Washington Way, Richland, WA 99352
(509) 943-5321   *M-F–10-5*

✪ 2,000 ▢ 10
　　▢ 75 ✎ 75 ▤ 300+ ☕ 50 ✂ 20 ✴ 30 ▥ 10
　　CA   *V M A D*

²⁸Friends and Company
4454 California Ave SW, Seattle, WA 98116
(206) 932-3891   *M-F–10-8 Sa–10-6 Su–11-5*

✪ 5,000 ▢ 45 M C S
　　▢ 100 ✎ 275+ ▤ 100 ☕ 50 ✂ 30 ✴ 20 ✪ 700 ▥ 10
　　C D CA SC N   *V M OSC*

²⁹Impress Rubber Stamps
Westlake Ctr, #310, 400 Pine St, Seattle, WA 98101
(206) 621-1878   *M-Sa–9:30-8 Su–11-6*

✪ 20,000 ▢ 100+ M C S
　　▢ 75 ✎ 200 ▤ 100 ☕ 50 ✂ 50 ✴ 75 ▥ 50
　　C D N   *V M*

³⁰Monkey Love Rubber Stamps
623 Queen Anne Ave N, Seattle, WA 98109
(206) 283-7897   *Tu-F–11-7 Sa,Su–12-5*

✪ 15,000 ▢ 100+ C S
　　▢ 250 ✎ 250 ▤ 250 ☕ 100 ✂ 50 ✴ 100 ▥ 30
　　C D N DC   *V M OSC*

³¹Paper Cat Rubber Stamps
218 1st Ave S, Seattle, WA 98104
(206) 623-3636   *M-Sa–9-6:15 Su–11-5*

✪ 30,000 ▢ 100+ S
　　▢ 275+ ✎ 275+ ▤ 200 ☕ 30 ✂ 50 ✴ 150+ ✪ 500 ▥ 25
　　D   *V M D OSC*

³²Stampola
7320 Greenwood Ave N, Seattle, WA 98103
(206) 706-7448   *M-Sa–11-6*

✪ 3,000 ⬛ 1 M C S
   ⬜150 ✐ 200 ▤ 20 ♒ 10 ✂ 50 ✪ 50 📖 5
   C D CA N   *V M OSC*

³³The Paper Zone
1216 3rd Ave, Seattle, WA 98101
(206) 682-7370   *M-F–8-6*

✪ 2,000 ⬛ 10 S *100's of papers for stamping*
   ▤ 300+
   C D CA   *V M A D OSC*

³⁴The Paper Zone
1911 1st Ave S, Seattle, WA 98134
(206) 682-8644   *M-F–8-7 Sa–10-5 Su–12-5*

✪ 2,000 ⬛ 10 S *100's of papers for stamping*
   ⬜50 ✐ 275+ ▤ 300+ ♒ 20 ✂ 75+ ✖ 50 ✪ 500 📖 30
   C D CA   *V M A D OSC*

³⁵Stamp-Til-U-Drop!
104 W Naches, Ste A, Selah, WA 98942
(509) 697-6887   *M-F–9-6 Sa–10-4*

✪ 2,000 ⬛ 20 C S
   ⬜100 ✐ 100 ▤ 300+ ♒ 30 ✂ 20 ✖ 10 ✪ 50 📖 30
   C D CA N DC   *V M OSC*

³⁶Rubber Stamp Merchant
990 E Washington, Ste E-100, Sequim, WA 98382
(360) 681-3173   *M-F–10-7 Su-12-4*

✪ 7,000 ⬛ 15 C S
   ⬜100 ✐ 150 ▤ 100 ♒ 50 ✂ 50 ✖ 100 📖 15
   C D CA N DC   *V M A D OSC*

³⁷The Paper Zone
15915 Westminster Way N, Shoreline, WA 98133
(206) 365-0558   M-F–8-6 Sa–10-5 Su–12-5

✪ 2,000 ⊠ 10 S *100's of papers for stamping*
   ⬜ 50 ✐ 275+ ▤ 300+ ☒ 20 ✂ 75+ ▩ 50 ✪ 500 ▥ 30
   C D CA   V M A D OSC

³⁸The Learning Tree
Kitsap Pl, 10300 Silverdale Way NW, Silverdale, WA 98383
(360) 692-5411   M-F–10-6 Sa–10-5 Su–12-4

✪ 500 ⊠ 10
   ⬜ 25 ✐ 25 ▤ 50 ☒ 20 ✂ 20 ▩ 10 ✪ 100 ▥ 20
   DC   V M D

³⁹The Stamp Box
1012 First St, Snohomish, WA 98290
(360) 568-7774   M-Sa–10-5 Su–12-4

✪ 3,000 ⊠ 100+ C S *India wood printing blocks*
   ⬜ 275+ ✐ 275+ ▤ 100 ☒ 30 ✂ 50 ▩ 50 ✪ 200 ▥ 70+
   C D CA N   V M D OSC

⁴⁰Gone Stamp'n
N 1510 Argonne Rd, Ste 4-D, Spokane, WA 99212
(509) 921-1205   M-F–10-6:30 Sa-10-5

✪ 3,000 ⊠ 80 S *Large variety of papers*
   ⬜ **100** ✐ **100** ▤ **150** ☒ **75** ✂ **50** ▩ **150+** ✪ **200** ▥ **30**
   C D CA SC N DC   V M OSC

⁴¹Kaleidoscope Stamping & Scrapping & Stuff
University City Mall, 10502 E Sprague Ave, Spokane, WA 99206
(509) 893-9404   M-F–10-7 Sa–10-6 Su–11-5

✪ 10,000 ⊠ 90 C S
   ⬜ 250 ✐ 275+ ▤ 300+ ☒ 50 ✂ 75+ ▩ 100 ✪ 1,000 ▥ 70+
   C D CA SC N DC HP   V M A D OSC

In Spokane, Washington it's
THE RUBBER STAMP STORE™
For the Artist in You!™

- Thousands of Stamps
- Full range of Accessories & Papers
- Brass Templates & Stencils
- Scrapbooks/Stickers/Supplies
- Pergamano and Paper Crafting
- Classes and Demonstrations
  (Please call, write, or visit our web page for our current schedule)

When you come to Eastern Washington, be sure to visit the friendly folks at the Inland Northwest's favorite rubber stamp store!

Driving Directions:
Take I-90 exit 281 (Division St.)
then go 3½ miles north to
NORTHTOWN MALL
(Use the Division Street mall entrance.)

**Watch for
Our New
Location!**

Mail and Phone Orders Welcome
4750 N. Division St. #199
Spokane, WA 99207
(509) 489-8563
Visa/MC/Amex/Discover

Store Hours: Mon - Sat 10:00 a.m. - 9:00 p.m. Sun 10:00 a.m. - 6:00 p.m.

w w w . t h e r u b b e r s t a m p s t o r e . c o m

FREE STAMP: Bring this directory into the store and get one free stamp or brass template with the purchase of another stamp or brass template of equal or greater value. Limited to stock on hand. Cannot be combined with any other coupon or discount. One free stamp or stencil per customer and per directory. Valid through 12/31/99.

Date Used:

⁴²Northwest Business Stamp

5210 N Market St, Spokane, WA 99207
(509) 483-0308   *M-F–9-5*

♻ 2,000 ▱1 M C S
　　▭200 ✎100 📖100 ⚖50 ✂20 🎨30 📖5
　　C D CA SC N DC　　　　　*V M A D OSC*

⁴³The Rubber Stamp Store

NorthTown Mall, #199, 4750 N Division, Spokane, WA 99207
(509) 489-8563   *M-Sa–10-9 Su–10-6*

♻ 15,000 ▱100+ C S
　　▭150 ✎275+ 📖250 ⚖100 ✂75+ 🎨150+ ♻1,000 📖25
　　C D CA N DC　　　　*V M A D OSC*

⁴⁴The Stamp Jeannie

923 E Hoffman, Spokane, WA 99207
(509) 487-9842   *M-Sa–10-5:30*

♻ 3,000 ▱100+ S *Stamp & scrapbooking supplies*
　　▭100 ✎200 📖150 ⚖150+ ✂50 🎨75 ♻100 📖70+
　　C D CA N DC　　　　*V M A D OSC*

⁴⁵Just Plain Fun

1027 Regents Blvd, Tacoma, WA 98466
(253) 565-2495   *Tu-F–10-6 Th–10-8 Sa–10-5 Su–1-5*

♻ 10,000 ▱100+ C S
　　▭275+ ✎275+ 📖200 ⚖50 ✂50 🎨150+ ♻300 📖50
　　D CA N DC　　　　　*V M A D OSC*

⁴⁶The Paper Zone

3304 S 23rd St, #C-2, Tacoma, WA 98405
(253) 572-5157   *M-F–8-9:30 Sa–9-8 Su–9-6*

♻ 3,000 ▱10 S *100's of papers for stamping*
　　▭50 ✎275+ 📖300+ ⚖20 ✂75+ 🎨50 ♻500 📖30
　　C D CA　　　　　*V M A D OSC*

⁴⁷Impress Rubber Stamps
120 Andover Park E, Ste 140, Tukwila, WA 98188
(206) 901-9101   *M-F–9:30-9 Sa–9:30-6 Su–11-5*

✪ 30,000 ⊠ 100+ M C S
⬚75 ✐200 ▯100 ≗50 ✂50 ✸75 📖50
   C D N   *V M*

⁴⁸The Paper Zone
120 Andover Park E, Ste 100, Tukwila, WA 98188
(206) 242-0255   *M-F–8-7 Sa–10-6 Su–11-5*

✪ 2,000 ⊠ 10 S *100's of papers for stamping*
⬚50 ✐275+ ▯300+ ≗20 ✂75+ ✸50 ✪500 📖30
   C D CA   *V M A D OSC*

⁴⁹The Paper Zone
6718-A NE 4th Plain Blvd, Vancouver, WA 98661
(360) 906-1644   *M-F–8-6 Sa–10-5 Su–12-5*

✪ 2,000 ⊠ 10 S *100's of papers for stamping*
⬚50 ✐275+ ▯300+ ≗20 ✂75+ ✸50 ✪500 📖30
   C D CA   *V M A D OSC*

⁵⁰Imagine That!
6 S Wenatchee, Wenatchee, WA 98801
(509) 662-8697   *M-F–10-6 Sa–10-5 Su–12-4*

✪ 2,000 ⊠ 50 S
⬚150 ✐275+ ▯100 ≗30 ✂15 ✸30 ✪50 📖70+
   C D CA SC N DC   *V M A D OSC*

⁵¹Pickle Papers
204 N Mission St, Wenatchee, WA 98801
(509) 665-8661   *M-F–10-6 Sa–11-5*

✪ 1,000 ⊠ 25 C S
⬚100 ✐75 ▯150 ≗50 ✂50 ✸10 ✪200 📖15
   C N   *V M OSC*

⁵²Paper Station
10 N Front St, Yakima, WA 98901
(509) 575-1633   *M-Sa–10-5:30*

✪ 3,000 ⊠ 25 S
   ⬜75 ✐200 📰150 🍴10 ✂15 🏥30 ✪1,000 📖5
   D CA DC   V M A D OSC

⁵³The Rubber Genie
1101 Pleasant Ave, Yakima, WA 98902
(509) 577-8847   *Tu-Sa–10-5:30*

✪ 3,000 ⊠ 60
   ⬜100 ✐275+ 📰150 🍴50 ✂30 🏥50 📖10
   C D CA SC N   V M A OSC

PASSPORT

WISCONSIN

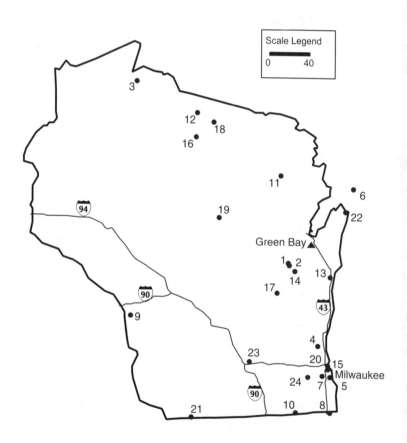

Scale Legend

0   40

3

12
18
16

11

6
22

19

Green Bay

1 2
14
13
17

43

90

9

4

23
20 15
Milwaukee
24 7 5
90
10 8

21

¹Oscar's Rubber Stamp Headquarters

Across from the Fox River Mall, 817 N Casaloma Dr, Appleton, WI 54915

(920) 731-4464   *M-Sa–9:30-9 Su–10-5*

✪ 30,000 ▱ 100+ M C S
　　▢ 275+ ✐ 275+ ▦ 300+ ☖ 150+ ✂ 75+ ▩ 100 ✪ 3,000+ ▱ 50
　　C D CA SC N DC   *V M D OSC*

²Oscar's Rubber Stamp Headquarters

Paper Valley Hotel, 333 W College Ave, Appleton, WI 54911

(920) 733-0030   *M-Su–9:30-9*

✪ 7,000 ▱ 25 M C S
　　▢ 275+ ✐ 275+ ▦ 300+ ☖ 150+ ✂ 75+ ▩ 100 ✪ 3,000+ ▱ 50
　　C D CA SC N DC   *V M D OSC*

³Northern Lights Stained Glass

723 9th Ave W, Ashland, WI 54806

(715) 682-4777   *M-F–12-5 Sa–9-12*

✪ 1,000 ▱ 10
　　▢ 25 ✐ 50 ▦ 20 ☖ 30 ✂ 10 ▩ 30 ▱ 3
　　C D HP   *OSC*

⁴Stampin' Cedarburg
W63 N698 Washington Ave, Cedarburg, WI 53012
(414) 375-5052   *M-Sa–10-5 Su–12-5*

✪ 30,000 ▨ 100+ C S
   ☐ 100 ✎ 200 📖 50 ⧗ 100 ✂ 20 ⊠ 150+ ✪ 500 📖 10
   C D CA SC N DC   *V M A D OSC*

⁵Cudahy News & Hobby Center
4758 S Packard Ave, Cudahy, WI 53110
(414) 769-1500   *M-F–9:30-8 Sa–9-5*

✪ 2,000 ▨ 20 S
   ☐ 50 ✎ 200 📖 50 ⧗ 30 ✂ 20 ⊠ 50 ✪ 50 📖 70+
   C D CA SC   *V M A D OSC*

⁶Oscar's Stamped On Main
Across From Founder's Sq, 4188 Main St, Fish Creek, WI 54212
(920) 868-1962   *M-Su–9-9*

✪ 20,000 ▨ 100+ M C S
   ☐ 275+ ✎ 275+ 📖 300+ ⧗ 150+ ✂ 75+ ⊠ 100 ✪ 3,000+ 📖 50
   C D CA SC N DC   *V M D OSC*

[7]Greenfield News & Hobby
6815 W Layton Ave, Greenfield, WI 53220
(414) 281-1800   *M-F–10-9 Sa–10-5*

✪ 2,000 ▱ 20 S
☐ 50 ✐ 200 ▤ 50 ☲ 30 ✂ 15 ❀ 25 ✪ 100 ▭ 70+
C D CA SC   *V M A D OSC*

[8]Stampfastic, Inc
5722 75th St (Hwy 50), Kenosha, WI 53142
(414) 697-7695   *M-Sa–10-5:00*

✪ 30,000 ▱ 100+ C S
☐ 150 ✐ 275+ ▤ 100 ☲ 100 ✂ 75+ ✪ 3,000+ ▭ 20
C D CA   *V M D OSC*

[9]Stamp 'n Hand
200 S 4th St, La Crosse, WI 54601
(608) 784-1234   *M-Sa–9:30-5:30 Th–9:30-8 Su–12-4*

✪ **50,000+** ▱ **100+** S
☐ **275+** ✐ **275+** ▤ **300+** ☲ **150+** ✂ **75+** ❀ **150+** ✪ **300** ▭ **70+**
C D CA SC N DC   ***V M D OSC***

[10]Mary Kays Stamps
647 W Main, Lake Geneva, WI 53147
(414) 248-4195   *M-Sa–9:30-5 Su–11-5*

✪ 30,000 ▱ 60 M C S
☐ 275+ ✐ 275+ ▤ 150 ☲ 50 ✂ 75+ ❀ 150+ ✪ 200 ▭ 25
C D CA N DC   *V M OSC*

[11]Birchwood Gallery
15481 Commercial Rd, Ste E, Lakewood, WI 54138
(715) 276-6998   *W-M–10-5*

✪ 500 ▱ 1 M C S
☐ 100 ✐ 25 ▤ 30 ☲ 10 ✪ 100 ▭ 5
C D CA DC   *V M D OSC*

[12]Classic Stamping & More

at Peppers Place N, Hwy W Downtown, PO Box 118, Manitowish Waters, WI 54545

(715) 543-2677 *M-Sa–10-5 Su–10-2 (Jan-May: Th-Sa–10-5) +by appt*

✪ 10,000 ▨ 100+ M C S

☐ 275+ ✐ 275+ ▤ 300+ ♨ 100 ✄ 75+ ▩ 100 ✪ 100 ▥ 40

C D CA N DC *V M OSC*

[13]Sue's Stamp Garden

814 Washington, Manitowoc, WI 54220

(920) 682-8578 *M-Th–9-5:30 F–9-8 Sa–9-3*

✪ 3,000 ▨ 70 S

☐ 100 ✐ 100 ▤ 250 ♨ 50 ✄ 30 ▩ 100 ✪ 100 ▥ 15

C D CA SC N DC HP *V M A D OSC*

[14]The Stamp Patch

1008-A Appleton Rd, (Appleton area) Menasha, WI 54952

(920) 720-0020 *M,Tu–10-6 W-F–10-8 Sa–10-5*

✪ 10,000 ▨ 100+ C S

☐ 150 ✐ 275+ ▤ 100 ♨ 75 ✄ 20 ▩ 150+ ✪ 200 ▥ 70+

C D CA SC DC *V M D OSC*

[15]Palette Shop Inc

342 N Water St, Milwaukee, WI 53202

(414) 272-3780 *M-F–8-5:30 W–8-7:30 Sa–9-5:30*

✪ 500 ▨ 25 S

☐ 50 ✐ 200 ▤ 100 ♨ 100 ✄ 50 ▩ 100 ✪ 200 ▥ 30

C D SC N DC *V M A D OSC*

[16]Classic Stamping & More

at Peppers Place S, 209 W Chicago St, Ste C, Minocqua, WI 54548

(715) 358-9988 *Tu-Sa–10-5 M,W,F–10-8 Su–10-4 (Mar,Apr: W-Sa–10-5)*

✪ 7,000 ▨ 100+ M C S *Scrapbooking & Supplies*

☐ 275+ ✐ 275+ ▤ 300+ ♨ 100 ✄ 75+ ▩ 150+ ✪ 200 ▥ 40

C D CA N DC *V M OSC*

¹⁷Creative Imagining
2080 W 9th Ave, Oshkosh, WI 54904
(920) 232-1680   *M-F–8-6 Sa–9-1*

✪ 10,000 ▨ 5 M C S *Rent a stamp program*
  ☐275+ ✐275+ ▤150 ♨50 ✂75+ ☐5
  C D CA N DC   *V M A D*

¹⁸Pastimes Gift Shop
441 Main St, Sayner, WI 54560
(715) 542-3837   *M-Su–9-5*

✪ 2,000 ▨ 35 S
  ☐25 ✐50 ▤30 ♨30 ✂15 ▨50 ☐3
  C D DC   *V M OSC*

¹⁹The Stamp Shoppe
4111 Schofield Ave, Ste 6, Schofield, WI 54476
(715) 355-6735   *Tu,W,F–10-6 Th–10-8 Sa–10-4*

✪ 5,000 ▨ 40 C S *We carry Stamps by Judith*
  ☐150 ✐200 ▤30 ♨30 ✂30 ▨150+ ✪50 ☐15
  C D CA N DC   *V M D OSC*

²⁰Coughlin & Co: Home of Inky Ideas
212 W Water St, Shullsburg, WI 53586
(608) 965-4979   *W-Sa–10-5 Su–12-5*

✪ 2,000 ▨ 15 C S
  ☐275+ ✐275+ ▤200 ♨150+ ✂30 ▨50 ✪1,000 ☐25
  C D CA N   *V M OSC*

²¹Palette Shop Inc
1325 E Capitol Dr, Shorewood, WI 53211
(414) 272-3780   *M–9-7:30 Tu-Th–9-6:30 F,Sa–9-5:30 Su–12-4
(Jun-Aug: Sa-9-3, closed Su)*

✪ 500 ▨ 25 S
  ☐25 ✐25 ▤50 ♨50 ✂50 ▨100 ✪100 ☐25
  C D CA SC N DC   *V M A D OSC*

²²Oscar's Door County Rubber Stamps

Historical Jefferson Street Shops, 751 Jefferson St, Sturgeon Bay, WI 54235

(920) 746-9080   *M-Sa–10-5 Su–11-4*

✪ 20,000 ▨ 100+ M C S

    ▭150 ✐275+ ▤300+ ⌛100 ✄75+ ✠100 ✪1,000 📖50

      C D CA SC N DC HP   *V M D OSC*

²³Country Charm Rubber Stamps

2087 McCoy Rd, Sun Prairie, WI 53590

(608) 825-2750   *M-F–10-8 Sa–10-5:30 Su–12-5*

✪ 12,000 ▨ 80 C S

    ▭200 ✐250 ▤150 ⌛100 ✄75+ ✠150+ 📖25

      C D CA SC N DC   *V M D OSC*

²⁴The Stamper's Lodge

N4 W 22496 Bluemound Rd, Waukesha, WI 53186

(414) 896-2131   *Tu-Sa–10-5:30 Su–12-5*

✪ 5,000 ▨ 10 C S

    ▭100 ✐275+ ▤200 ⌛75 ✄15 ✠75 ✪50 📖15

      C D CA SC N DC   *V M OSC*

WYOMING

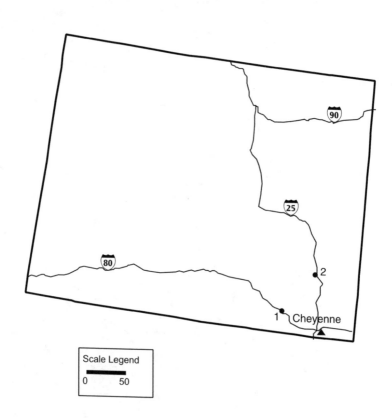

Scale Legend

0   50

¹The Other Store

200 S 2nd St, Laramie, WY 82070
(307) 742-7324   *M-Sa–9:30-6 Su–12-4*

✪ 1,000 ⊡ 10 S
  ⬜ 200 ✏ 275+ 📗 300+ ⚲ 50 ✂ 30 ▨ 150+ ✿ 500 📖 20
  C D CA DC   *V M A D OSC*

²Deer Creek Stamp Co

1555 South St, Wheatland, WY 82201
(307) 322-4439   *M,Tu–6-8 W–11-5 Th,F–11-8 Sa–11-4 Su–12-3*

✪ 2,000 ⊡ 70 M C
  ⬜ 150 ✏ 200 📗 100 ⚲ 100 ✂ 50 ▨ 50 📖 10
  C D CA SC N DC HP   *V M OSC*

ALBERTA

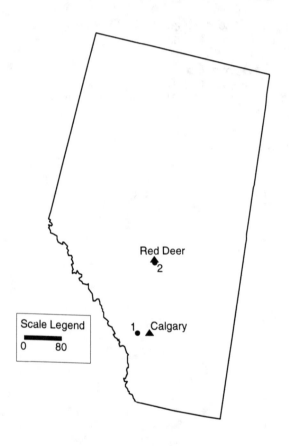

Red Deer
◆2

Scale Legend
━━━
0   80

1.● ▲Calgary

¹Stamp It
105830 8th St, Riverstone, Canmore, AB T1W 2B7
(403) 678-6563   *M-Sa–10-6 Su–12-5 (May-Sept: M-Sa–10-8
F–10-9 Su–12-8)*

☺ 3,000 ⌂ 30 C S
⬜75 ✐75 📄100 ⚗50 ✂15 ⊞100 📖25
C D CA DC HP   *V M A*

²Stamper's Delight
#5 4801-51 Ave, Red Deer, AB T4N 4H
(403) 340-0539   *M-F–10-5:30 Sa–10-5*

☺ 3,000 ⌂ 50 M C S
⬜200 ✐275+ 📄100 ⚗50 ✂75+ ⊞150+ ☺100 📖25
C D CA N   *V M*

BRITISH COLUMBIA

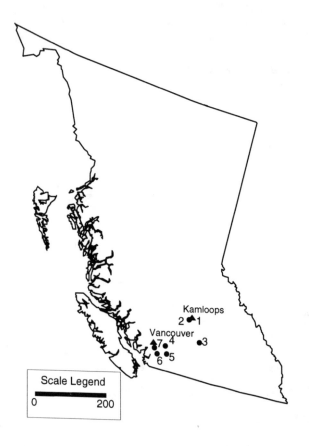

¹Impressions Stamp Gallery
426 Victoria St, Kamloops, BC V2C 2A7
(250) 372-1688   *M-Sa–9:30-5 (Jul--Aug: M-Sa–9:30-9)*

✪ 3,000 ◳ 45 C S
   □ 50 ✎ 100 ▤ 300+ ☙ 50 ✂ 50 ▨ 20 ✪ 50 ▢ 30
   C D CA SC N DC   *V M OSC*

²Sam's Stamping Grounds
Thompson Park Mall, 18B-450 Lansdowne St, Kamloops, BC V2C 1Y3
(250) 851-4474   *M-Sa–9:30-5:30 Th,F–9:30-9:00 Su–12-5*

✪ 3,000 ◳ 5 C *Canadian Stamps!*
   □ 75 ✎ 75 ▤ 300+ ☙ 30 ✂ 75+ ▨ 50 ✪ 1,000 ▢ 20
   C D CA SC DC   *V M*

³Stamper's Magic
1559 Ellis St, Kelowna, BC V1Y 2A7
(250) 717-5611   *M-F–9-5 Sa–9:30-4*

✪ 3,000 ◳ 5 C S
   □ 275+ ✎ 50 ▤ 300+ ☙ 150+ ✂ 7 ▢ 3
   C D CA DC HP   *V M*

⁴Great Canadian Stamp
19705 Fraser Hwy, #214, Langley, BC V3A 7E9
(604) 460-7244   *M-Sa–9:30-6 W-F–9:30-9 Su–11-5*

✪ 1,000 ◳ 1 M C S
   □ 200 ✎ 100 ▤ 100 ☙ 50 ✂ 20
   C D CA SC N DC HP   *V M A*

⁵Great Canadian Stamp
11455 201A St, Unit 1, Maple Ridge, BC V2X 0Y3
(604) 460-7244   *M-F–10-5:30 Sa–10-4*

✪ **1,000** ◳ **1 M C**
   □ **200** ✎ **100** ▤ **100** ☙ **50** ✂ **20**
   C D CA SC DC HP   ***V M A OSC***

⁶The World of Stamps

12115 1st Ave, Richmond, BC V7E 3M1
(604) 274-7827   *M-Sa–10:30-5 Su–1-5*

✪ 3,000 ⊠ 40 C S

☐ 150 ✐ 200 ▤ 300+ ⚱ 30 ✂ 50 ▦ 100 ✪ 100 📖 30
C D CA N HP   *V M OSC*

⁷Great Canadian Stamp

At The Bay, 674 Granville St, Vancouver, BC V6C 1Z6
(604) 689-2232   *M-W–7:30-6 Th,F–7:30-9 Sa–8:30-7*

✪ 1,000 ⊠ 1 M C

☐ 200 ✐ 100 ▤ 100 ⚱ 50 ✂ 20
C D CA SC DC   *V M A OSC*

PASSPORT

ONTARIO

Scale Legend

0   200

2 ●▲
Ottawa

Toronto
5 ●
6 3
4 ●

1 ●

¹Stamp Shack
Galleria London, 355 Wellington St, London, ON N6A 3N1
(519) 673-1823   M-W–10-6 Th,F–10-9 Sa–9:30-6 Su–12-5

✪ 3,000 ▱ 50 M C S
　　▭275+ ✐150 ▥250 ≋150+ ✂20 ▨100 📖15
　　C D CA SC N HP   V M D OSC

²Heather's Stamping Haven
250 Greenbank Rd, Nepean, ON K2H 8X4
(613) 726-0030   M-F–10-6 Th–10-8 Sa–10-5

✪ 2,000 ▱ 50 M C S "Microfleur" flower press
　　▭150 ✐275+ ▥300+ ≋50 ✂20 ▨30 📖30
　　C D CA N DC   V M

³The Brown Paper Wrapper
#5 67 Bronte Rd, Oakville, ON L6L 3B7
(905) 469-8655   Tu-Th–10-6 F–10-8 Sa–10-5 Su–12-5

✪ 5,000 ▱ 40 C S
　　▭150 ✐275+ ▥150 ≋50 ✂50 ▨50 📖25
　　C D CA N   V M

⁴The Rubber Stamp Store
17 Main St, St Catharines, ON L2N 4T5
(905) 938-1235   M-Sa–10-5:30

✪ 7,000 ▱ 30 C S
　　▭150 ✐200 ▥100 ≋100 ✂75+ ▨100 📖25
　　C D CA DC HP   V M A

⁵Great Impressions
207 Queen's Quay W, Box 80, Toronto, ON M5J 1A7
(416) 203-0433   M-Su–10-6 (May-Aug: M-Sa–10-9 Su–10-6)

✪ 7,000 ▱ 35 C S
　　▭200 ✐200 ▥50 ≋50 ✂50 ▨100 ✪50 📖30
　　C D CA SC   V M A

⁶Stamper's Studio

2255 Queen St, #B, Toronto, ON M4E 1G3
(416) 690-4446   *Tu,W,Sa–10-6   Th,F–10-8   Su–1-5*

✪ 5,000   ⊠ 40   C

⬜100   ✐275+   ▤300+   ⌛150+   ✂20   ▨75   📖50
C D CA N DC   V M

⁷The Rubber Stamp General Store

61 Jackson Ave, Toronto, ON M8X 2J7
(416) 231-0583   *Appt only, call for location*

✪ 5,000   ⊠ 25   M C

⬜25   ✐100   ▤30   ⌛20   ✂7   ▨50   📖15
C D CA N HP   V M

PASSPORT

QUEBEC

Montreal
▲ ●1

Scale Legend
0 ━━━━━━ 200

¹Les Ateliers Du Chat Bleu

351 Blain, Mont Saint-Hilaire, PQ J3H 3B4
(514) 446-5253   *M-F–10-5 Sa–11-5*

✪ 500 ◩ 10 M
☐ 50 ✐ 150 ▤ 200 ♟ 30 ✂ 30 ✹ 100 📖 5
C D CA N DC   *V M*

ENGLAND

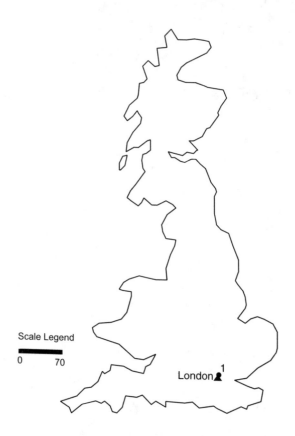

Scale Legend

0   70

London [1]

¹**Blade Rubber**

2 Neal's Yard, Covent Garden, London WC2H 9DP
(171) 379-7391   *M-Sa−10:30-6*

✪ 2,000 ⊡ 20 M C
   ▢75 ✐150 ▤150 ⚲50 ✂50 ✪100 📖10
   C D CA   *V*

"TRAVELER'S CHEQUE" DISCOUNT COUPONS

The eight discount coupons following this page are each good for a $1.00 discount on purchases of $15.00 or more in stamps or accessories at participating stores.

These coupons are valid under the following conditions:

- Limit one coupon per person per store
- Your name is signed on the front of the coupon
- Only original "Traveler's Cheques will be accepted (no photocopies or other reproductions)
- Coupon is not valid with other discounts
- Offer is good until January 1, 2000

To make them easy to remove, the coupons are perforated both along the binding edge and between each coupon.

$1 Cornucopia Press Traveler's Cheque **$1**

ONE DOLLAR discount
on $15 or more purchase
at participating stores.

_____

$1 Cornucopia Press Traveler's Cheque **$1**

ONE DOLLAR discount
on $15 or more purchase
at participating stores.

_____

$1 Cornucopia Press Traveler's Cheque **$1**

ONE DOLLAR discount
on $15 or more purchase
at participating stores.

_____

$1 Cornucopia Press Traveler's Cheque **$1**

ONE DOLLAR discount
on $15 or more purchase
at participating stores.

_____

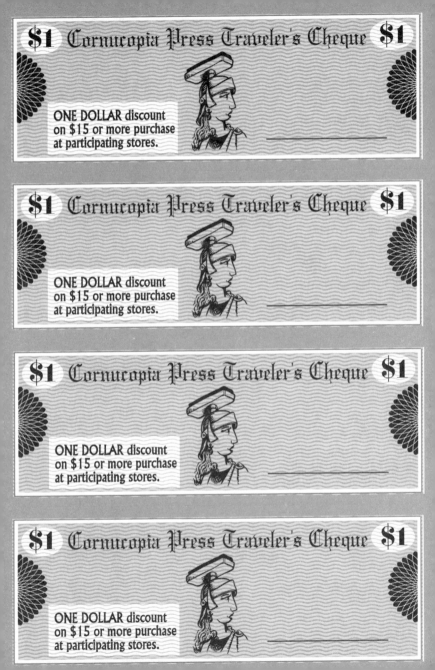

STAMPS USED IN THE BOOK

FRONT COVER
Lizard-Ruby Red Rubber
Leaf-The Moon Rose
Safety pin-Paper Source
Anchor-A La Art
Air mail letter-Fishbone Graphics
Hearts-Fishbone Graphics
Broken record-Leavenworth Jackson
Keyboard-Magenta
Band-aid-Toomuchfun Rubber Stamps
Scared chicken-Bizzaro
Leonardo's man-Stamp Out Cute
Firecracker-The Cottage Stamper. Inc
Light bulb-Gumbo Graphics
Watch-Gumbo Graphics

BACK COVER
House-Stamp Cabana
Plane & banner-Stamp Cabana
Sun-Stamp Cabana
Trees & shrubs-Stamp Cabana
Sky-Stamp Cabana
Picket fence-Stamp Cabana
Moon-Handle with Love & Co

Other cover images-Hand-drawn by Leonard Rifas

Maps-Business Map

Vehicles-Image Club Mini-Pics Vehicles

Other Images-Art Parts clip art

NEW STORE LISTINGS

If you are familiar with other stores, please let us know about them. We'd love to include those stores in future editions of *A Traveler's Guide to Rubber Stamp Stores* and in our *Rubber Stamp Sourcebook.*.

Store Name_____

Address_____

_____

City_____State_____Zip_____

Country_____Phone_____

INFORMATION

If you would like information about new Cornucopia Press publications as they appear, fill out the information below and mail to: Cornucopia Press, 4739 University Way NE, Ste 1610, Seattle, WA 98105

Name_____

Address_____

_____

City_____State_____Zip_____

Country_____Phone_____

RUBBER STAMP SOURCEBOOK
The Big Book of Everything in Rubber Stamps

Projects

Basic Techniques
3-D Effects
Stamping in Food
Stamp Jewelry
Papermaking
Scrapbooking
Handmade Books

2,500 Designs

Resources

Stamp Stores (1,000)
Stamp Manufacturers (250)
Accessory Suppliers (300)
Annotated Bibliography
  (500 books)
Stamps by Category
  (1,200 listings)

Images from
100 Catalogs

350+ Pages

Only $21.95 U.S. + shipping
See next page for ordering information.

ORDER FORM

If you can't find our books at your favorite bookstore or rubber stamp store you may order directly from:

Cornucopia Press   Phone (206) 528-8120
4739 University Way NE   Fax (206) 528-8106
Suite 1610-D   ORDERS ONLY:
Seattle, WA 98105   (800) 790-3878
USA   Fax (800) 790-3879

Name_____

Address_____

_____

City_____State____Zip_____

Country_____Day Phone_____

Please send me:

_____Traveler's Guide to Rubber Stamp Stores ($9.95 + S/H)

_____Rubber Stamp Sourcebook ($21.95 + S/H)

SHIPPING (all prices are in U.S. dollars and per book)

	TRAVELER'S GUIDE	SOURCEBOOK
Surface rate within U.S.	$1.50	$2.50
First Class Mail within U.S.	$2.25	$4.00
Surface rate outside U.S.	$2.00	$4.00

Purchase orders, STOP orders and credit card orders all accepted.

Wholesale orders also available. Inquire for prices.

Sales Tax–Washington residents add 8.6%.

Satisfaction Guaranteed–Full refund if dissatisfied for any reason.